A BRIEF NARRATIVE OF THE
Fourth Tennessee Cavalry Regiment

WHEELER'S CORPS, ARMY OF TENNESSEE

By GEORGE B. GUILD

NASHVILLE, TENN.
1913

Notice

In many older books, foxing (or discoloration) occurs and, in some instances, print lightens with wear and age. Reprinted books, such as this, often duplicate these flaws, notwithstanding efforts to reduce or eliminate them. The pages of this reprint have been digitally enhanced and, where possible, the flaws eliminated in order to provide clarity of content and a pleasant reading experience.

A Brief Narrative of the Fourth Tennessee Cavalry Regiment, Wheeler's Corps, Army of Tennessee

Originally published
Nashville, Tennessee
1913

Reprinted by:

Janaway Publishing, Inc.
732 Kelsey Ct.
Santa Maria, California 93454
(805) 925-1038
www.janawaygenealogy.com

2012

ISBN: 978-1-59641-289-7

Made in the United States of America

Dedication

*To those comrades "who went with us but came
not back again," many of whom are sleep-
ing in their blankets in unknown
graves on the battle fields
where they fell*

The rough board that perhaps a comrade placed at the head to direct the footsteps of inquiring friends has long since rotted down; and the little mound they spread above their soldier breast has been leveled by the plowshare or the long years that have passed since then. But there the wild flower sheds its sweetest perfume to the morning air, and the song bird warbles its lay to the setting sun, and at night the stars of heaven, as they climb the Milky Way, look down and grow brighter as they pass.

CONTENTS

	PAGE
INTRODUCTORY	7
I. ORGANIZATION AND EARLY MOVEMENTS	9

Outpost Duty at Franklin, Tenn.—Battle of Murfreesboro—Retreat to Shelbyville.

II. FROM FORT DONELSON TO CHICKAMAUGA 16

Fort Donelson—Woodbury, Tenn.—Trousdale's Ferry on Caney Fork River—Resisting Rosecrans's Advance on Shelbyville and Tullahoma—Bragg's Retreat to Chattanooga — Wheeler's Cavalry at Rome, Ga.—Battle of Chickamauga.

III. WHEELER'S RAID INTO MIDDLE TENNESSEE IN 1863.. 35
IV. IN EAST TENNESSEE............................ 49

Return to the Army of Tennessee at Missionary Ridge—Report of Lieutenant Colonel Anderson on the Battle of Chickamauga—Battles of Lookout Mountain and Orchard Knob—Missionary Ridge and Ringgold, Ga.

V. CAMPAIGNING IN GEORGIA...................... 57

Gen. Joseph E. Johnston Succeeds General Bragg as Commander in Chief—Remarks about General Bragg—General Sherman Advances on Dalton, Ga. —March to Atlanta, Ga.—Battles of Resaca and Kingston—New Hope Church—Kennesaw Mountain—Marietta and Atlanta—General Johnston Superseded by General Hood.

VI. GENERAL WHEELER'S CAPTURE OF THE COMMANDS OF GENERALS MCCOOK AND STONEMAN.......... 69

Raid of General Wheeler into Tennessee in 1864 —Behind the Lines.

VII. IN TENNESSEE, VIRGINIA, AND HARASSING SHERMAN 97

March through East Tennessee—Battle of Saltville, Va.—Return to Atlanta, Ga.—Sherman's March to the Sea.

		PAGE
VIII.	THE SOUTH CAROLINA CAMPAIGN................ Remarks about General Hood—Battle of Aiken, S. C.—Battle of Fayetteville, N. C.	112
IX.	IN NORTH CAROLINA............................ Change in Brigade Officers—Gen. Joseph E. Johnston Succeeds General Hood and Assumes Command in North Carolina—Battle of Averyboro, N. C.—Bentonville, N. C.	125
X.	FURTHER MOVEMENTS IN NORTH CAROLINA, AND THE BEGINNING OF THE END..................... Reorganization of the Army at Smithfield, N. C.—General Johnston Ordered to Greensboro, N. C.—Meets Confederate States Officials—General Johnston Confers with General Sherman, and an Agreement Made to End the War.	136
XI.	THE END OF THE STRUGGLE...................... Surprise of the Army at Information of Surrender—Sherman-Johnston Capitulation Rejected at Washington—Another Agreement Looking to a Surrender on Terms Given General Lee at Appomattox—General Johnston's Farewell Address to the Army—General Wheeler's Address to the Cavalry.	143
XII.	CASUALTY LISTS	153
XIII.	GEN. JOSEPH E. JOHNSTON AND OTHER OFFICERS..	172
XIV.	AN ADDRESS AND A SPEECH.......................	185
XV.	A FEW FACTS FROM HISTORY.....................	195
XVI.	AFTER THE WAR.................................	206
XVII.	GENERAL BRAGG'S KENTUCKY CAMPAIGN IN 1862 (By Baxter Smith)...........................	211
XVIII.	MEMBERS OF THE REGIMENT NOW LIVING.........	239
	APPENDIX	257
	INDEX	262

INTRODUCTORY.

SINCE the surrender of the Confederate army, in the spring of 1865, I have been frequently asked by members of the Regiment to write its history. I have always promised, but have failed to comply till now I find myself attempting it forty-seven years afterwards. Many of those who survived the surrender have died. Some have removed to parts unknown, and a very few remain from whom I can obtain necessary information. So I am forced to write mostly from a personal recollection, without memorandum or note. This I regret; for it forces me to speak of some, while I have forgotten others equally as worthy of mention. I offer this as my apology for an imperfect record.

It has been my effort to write a narrative of my own Regiment. Necessarily it can be of but little interest to the public, although it embraces a cursory history of the Army of Tennessee, of which it was a part. I see that some repetition appears in its pages, growing out of a predisposition to emphasize some facts, which I ask you to excuse.

CHAPTER I.

ORGANIZATION AND EARLY MOVEMENTS.

THE Fourth Tennessee Cavalry did not assume regimental form until General Bragg had returned from his Kentucky campaign, in the fall of 1862. It was made up of detachments that had served under different commanders since the beginning of the war. At its organization Baxter Smith was made Colonel; Paul F. Anderson, Lieutenant Colonel; W. Scott Bledsoe, Major; J. A. Minnis, Adjutant; W. A. Rushing, Sergeant Major; Marcellus Grissim, Quartermaster, with R. O. McLean, Bob Corder, and John Price his assistants; Captain Bone, Commissary, with Lieut. J. A. Arnold and Captain McLean his assistants; Dr. W. T. Delaney, Surgeon, with Dr. Tom Allen his assistant; Rev. W. W. Hendrix, Chaplain; Sergeant Finney, Ordnance Officer; J. A. Stewart and James B. Nance, Regimental Buglers; Bob Gann and Bennett Chapman, Wagon Masters.

The commissioned officers of the companies were:

Company A.—Captain, D. W. Alexander; First Lieutenant, Rice McLean; Second Lieutenant, J. N. Orr; Third Lieutenant, Charles Beard. Recruited in Marshall County, Tenn.

Company B.—Captain, C. H. Ingles; First Lieutenant, Joe Massengale; Second Lieutenant, Joe Massengale; Third Lieutenant, G. W. Carmack. Recruited in Sullivan County, Tenn.

Fourth Tennessee Cavalry Regiment.

Company C.—Captains, Frank Cunningham* and George C. Moore; First Lieutenant, James Hogan; Second Lieutenant, R. S. Scruggs; Third Lieutenant, Samuel Scoggins. Recruited in Smith County, Tenn.

Company D.—Captain, J. M. Phillips; First Lieutenant, Bob Bone; Second Lieutenant, J. T. Barbee; Third Lieutenant, J. A. Arnold. Recruited in DeKalb and Wilson Counties, Tenn.

Company E.—Captain, H. A. Wyly; First Lieutenant, H. L. Preston; Second Lieutenant, W. S. Sullivan; Third Lieutenant, John Fathera. Recruited in Cannon County, Tenn.

Company F.—Captain, J. R. Lester; First Lieutenant, C. S. Burgess; Second Lieutenant, W. H. Phillips; Third Lieutenant, James Williamson. Recruited in Wilson County, Tenn.

Company G.—Captain, J. W. Nichol; First Lieutenant, Dave Youree; Second Lieutenant, — McKnight; Third Lieutenant, J. A. Sagely. Recruited in Cannon and Rutherford Counties, Tenn.

Company H.—Captain, Sam Glover; Lieutenants, Green, Light, William Gaut, and William Fields. Recruited in Hamilton County and Bridgeport, Ala.

Company I.—Captain, Bob Bledsoe; Lieutenants, William Hildreth, J. W. Storey, Foster Bowman, and Elliott. Recruited in Fentress County, Tenn.

Company K.—Captain, Jim Britton; Lieutenants, W. Corbett and Dewitt Anderson. Recruited in Wilson, Sumner, and Davidson Counties, Tenn.

Company L.†—Captain, J: J. Parton; Lieutenants, Henry, Russell, and Tillery. Recruited in Knox County, Tenn.

---

*Resigned soon after organization of Regiment, and Lieut. George C. Moore succeeded him, serving till the surrender.

†This Company was not attached to the Regiment till just before the battle of Chickamauga. It had been the escort of General McGowan, who resigned, and it reported to the Fourth Tennessee, serving till the surrender. It was a very small company.

The Regiment was assigned to a brigade composed of the Eighth Texas, Eleventh Texas, First Kentucky, and Fourth Tennessee Regiments and Malone's Alabama Battalion, Col. Tom Harrison as Senior Colonel commanding the brigade, Maj. Gen. John A. Wharton commanding the division (Gen. Joe Wheeler's Corps, Army of Tennessee), and sent to Franklin, Tenn., on outpost duty. General Bragg, with the infantry force, was at Murfreesboro, confronting General Rosecrans's Federal army at Nashville.

It is well enough to state here that there were two Fourth Tennessee Cavalry Regiments in the army—Colonel Stearns's Fourth Tennessee and Colonel Smith's Fourth Tennessee. They had been serving in different departments of the army, one under General Forrest and the other under General Wheeler, most of the time, and we did not know the fact until late in the war. Both had made character under that name, and each tacitly agreed to remain as they had been known, which they did. At the date of the organization of the Fourth Tennessee Cavalry Regiment it numbered one thousand men, rank and file, made up principally of stout, healthy, and vigorous young men. As stated, our first service as a regiment was at Franklin, on General Bragg's front and left flank, some twenty miles from Murfreesboro and eighteen miles from Nashville, where we were kept busy for some two months or more in picketing, scouting on all the roads leading toward Murfreesboro from Nashville, occasionally having some hot contests with the enemy, killing, wounding, and capturing some, and losing some ourselves. At one time we scouted toward Nashville in the night, and remained all day in the vicinity, expecting the enemy to come out, as was their custom, on foraging expeditions, which they failed to do. But before leaving we concluded to give them a closer dare. In the evening we came up the Charlotte Pike as far as what is now West Nashville, and, going up Richland Creek, we came in contact with a force of the enemy at Bosley Springs, and, charging them, drove them back to the Harding Pike, capturing some and pursuing the others to where the old penitentiary wall stood, on Church Street. We remained in line a short distance down the road till near sundown; but no enemy appearing, we repaired to our station at Franklin.

The enemy made frequent scouts in the neighborhood of Franklin, sometimes resulting in quite a battle. I remember that in one of these Captain McMillin, a brother of Ex-Governor McMillin, was killed. He was on a visit to some acquaintances in the Regiment, and went out with the Regiment to meet one of these scouts of the enemy.

In the latter part of December, 1862, Rosecrans marched on Murfreesboro. The Regiment skirmished with his advance till he reached the place.

Capt. J. R. Lester, of Company F, was desperately wounded in one of these skirmishes. We thought at the time that his wound was mortal, but he returned to his company in a few weeks, and served with them till the surrender at Greensboro, N. C. When Colonel Smith as Senior Colonel assumed the command of the brigade, Capt. J. R. Lester was made his Inspector General, and surrendered as such.

On reaching Murfreesboro we were placed on the right of our line on the Lebanon Pike, where General Bragg supposed the enemy would first attack; but changing his plans during the night, he attacked with his left flank about daylight. A terrific battle ensued here. It seems the enemy at the time was moving to attack Bragg from that flank, and the two armies unexpectedly met in deadly conflict. The battle raged in all its fury for hours. Charge after charge and countercharge was made time and again, with heavy losses on both sides. The Confederates, steadily advancing, gradually forced the enemy back, capturing many pieces of artillery and small arms, with many prisoners. Among the captured was General Willich and his German Brigade. Gen. Jim Rains, of the Confederate army, and General Sill, of the Federal army, were killed in one of these assaults. Before night the Federal army was forced back to the Nashville Pike, at right angles to the position they held when first attacked. The Confederates had gained a great victory. The loss of each was about equal—say, ten thousand. Six thousand Federal prisoners were captured, and several batteries of artillery, besides thousands of muskets and ammunition. The next morning every one expected the battle to be renewed, and were much disappointed that General Bragg did not follow up his advantage, instead of which he remained inactive for several days. In the meantime he ordered General Wheeler, with his cavalry corps, to the rear of General Rosecrans, toward Nashville. All along the way to La Vergne we were picking up prisoners, and everything indicated a defeat and rout of the enemy. At the latter place we came up with a long train of wagons moving toward Nashville with an escort of several thousand cavalry. We engaged them, and, after a considerable battle, they retreated. We captured and destroyed some two hundred wagons, some prisoners were taken, and a good many men on both sides were killed and wounded. Many of Rosecrans's men had reached Nashville, reporting that his army had been badly beaten. Still no movement had been made by General Bragg at Murfreesboro. The enemy had taken advantage of this inactivity by collecting together their broken columns and taking position on high ground on the banks of Stones River, and crowned it with a number of batteries—fifty-seven pieces—well protected, awaiting the movement of General Bragg. On the first day of January he attacked this well-fortified place of the enemy with the single division of General Breckenridge. After a most gallant assault by Breckenridge, he was repulsed with heavy loss. That night the cavalry of Wheeler occupied the works of the infantry when they withdrew toward Shelbyville. General Bragg, it seems, had sent off during this lull in movements all of his wounded and the prisoners he had taken. At daylight on the 2d of January, 1863, Wheeler's cavalry also withdrew, following the infantry toward Shelbyville. No pursuit was made. The Federals were as much surprised as the Confederates at the result, and it was sometime during the day before they could realize the fact of the withdrawal of Bragg's troops. Much adverse criticism was made of General Bragg's failure to take advantage of the victory he had obtained in the first days of the battle, and especially of the assault he made against the well-prepared works of the enemy, when it should have been with his entire army instead of a single division. Such was the opinion of the humblest soldier in his army.

CHAPTER II.

FROM FORT DONELSON TO CHICKAMAUGA.

GENERAL BRAGG upon reaching Shelbyville went regularly into camp, and remained there some three or four months drilling, recruiting, and strengthening his army. General Wheeler, with his corps, was on the front watching the movement of the Federal army at Murfreesboro, scouting all the approaches, with an occasional scrap with the enemy, sometimes approaching the dignity of a battle.

In January, 1863, Wheeler's Corps was ordered to Fort Donelson with a view of capturing the garrison stationed there. General Forrest was ordered up from West Tennessee to coöperate with Wheeler. On reaching the place, Wheeler made his arrangements to attack, and did attack the fortifications; but General Forrest refusing to coöperate, he was repulsed and the expedition was a failure. Wheeler lost quite a number of men. Col. Frank McNairy, a well-known citizen of Nashville, was killed in leading a charge. The weather was extremely cold. The streams were full of ice and the dirt roads were frozen hard, making it a matter of difficulty to pass over. Men and horses suffered greatly, as much as at any time during the war. On going back to Shelbyville, the Fourth Tennessee was detached and sent by General Bragg to Woodbury to relieve a portion of General Morgan's command under Captain Hutchison, who was killed in an engagement with the enemy the day before we reached there. He was a fine soldier, and his death was much regretted. His home was at Springfield, Tenn., where he is affectionately remembered. The Regiment was at Woodbury some weeks, during which time we had frequent battles with the enemy coming up from Murfreesboro, where the Federal army was still stationed. We lost quite a number of men, killed and wounded. In one of these engagements Colonel Smith received a saber cut, and would probably have been killed had not the bugler of the Regiment, J. A. Stuart, relieved the situation by a well-directed shot from his pistol. From Woodbury we were ordered over to Trousdale's Ferry, on the Caney Fork River. We went from there on a scout toward Nashville, and, turning off the Lebanon Pike, went to a point on the Cumberland River a mile above Edgefield Junction, where we waited, in ambush, for a train on the Louisville and Nashville Railroad to come in sight. We had a piece of artillery with us, commanded by Lieutenant White; and when a long train made its appearance, he opened on it, and about the first shot went into the steam chest of the engine, bringing the train to a stop in full view of our position. The train was loaded with horses; and after demolishing it and everything in sight, we retired.

18   Fourth Tennessee Cavalry Regiment.

Some of the men asked to be permitted to go over and get some of the horses; but Colonel Smith would not allow it, as he had another trip in contemplation, to wit: to go over to the Nashville and Chattanooga Railroad. Near Smyrna we captured a long train of cars full of officers and soldiers without firing a gun. The men were allowed to help themselves bountifully to the rich booty; and being paroled, the prisoners were permitted to pursue their journey toward Nashville on foot. From there we returned to our post at Trousdale's Ferry. In a short while thereafter Colonel Smith and Adjutant Minnis were captured by the enemy under the following circumstances: They had been across the river inspecting the picket posts on that side, and on their return to camp after dark they were captured by a scout of the enemy which had been piloted around the pickets by a Union man of that vicinity. As soon as it was ascertained, a squad from the picket post pursued them to the vicinity of Carthage, about seven miles. They came in view of the scouts with the prisoners, whom they managed to keep so exposed that the Confederates were afraid to fire at them for fear of killing Colonel Smith and Minnis. The writer was appointed to fill the place of Adjutant Minnis, and served in this capacity till the battle of Fayetteville, N. C., in February, 1865, when he was appointed Adjutant General of the brigade, and served and surrendered as such at Greensboro, N. C., April 26,

Fourth Tennessee Cavalry Regiment. 19

1865. We remained some days longer on the Caney Fork, till General Rosecrans commenced his movement against General Bragg, when we were ordered to Shelbyville. We reached there in time to resist the advance of the enemy, having some well-contested battles with them, in which a good many of our men were killed and wounded, and inflicting a like loss on the enemy. Here the greater part of Colonel Malone's Battalion, of Alabama, was captured, and we saw no more of them during the war.

When Rosecrans began his movement on Shelbyville with a heavy column, he sent a like column down the Chattanooga Railway toward Tullahoma. In order to meet this movement, General Bragg fell back to Tullahoma, where the two columns of the enemy were expected to concentrate.

The Army of Tennessee remained at Tullahoma some three or four weeks, during which time they were kept busy drilling, collecting supplies, recruiting, etc. The conscript law of the Confederate government was in full force, and Bragg received from this source quite an accession to his army. Some of these made as good soldiers as we had, but as a general thing they were a very uncertain quantity and would not do to depend on. In a short time General Rosecrans's army appeared before Tullahoma. It had been largely recruited and numbered double the strength of the Army of Tennessee. In one of the cavalry battles around Tullahoma that great soldier, Gen. James Starnes, had been killed. His death created quite a gloom, and, had he lived, he would certainly have won higher rank. Judge McLemore, of Franklin, succeeded to his command.

General Bragg began his retrograde movement toward Chattanooga in June (I think), very wisely concluding to draw the Federals farther from his base before risking another general engagement. General Wheeler covered his rear, which the enemy's cavalry assailed very vigorously, using their batteries freely. This continued until we passed over Cumberland Mountain, both armies losing quite a number in killed and wounded, some prisoners being taken. After passing the mountain a lull in the operations of both armies ensued. The Confederate infantry had passed on to Chattanooga. Wheeler's cavalry, reaching the Tennessee River, passed over the bridge at Bridgeport on the plank flooring that had been laid upon the girders. After reaching Shellmound, on the Nashville and Chattanooga Railroad, General Wheeler was ordered to go to Rome, Ga., with a view to recuperating his much-jaded cavalry horses. Here we remained for two months or more and had the only real rest that we got during our service in the army. Rome was then a pleasant little city of about five thousand inhabitants, surrounded by a rich and fertile country. Wheeler's Cavalry Corps numbered about five thousand, rank and file. The quartermasters of the respective regiments would buy a field of corn, move to it, and remain until it was exhausted, and then move on to another purchase. The horses would be fed on the corn, stalks and all, using a plentiful supply of salt, besides grazing them on grass for an hour or two each day. It was wonderful how they improved, and by the time we left there they looked as if they had been prepared for a State Fair.

The soldiers, too, were supplied with an abundance of substantial and wholesome rations. The strictest discipline prevailed. Drills were the order of the day, with both officers and privates, at least two hours each morning and evening. Prayer meetings and services by the respective chaplains were held regularly, were well attended, and many conversions took place. Drs. Bunting and Hendricks, our brigade and regimental chaplains, were kept busy and active in their duties, and we know that many lasting and substantial conversions were made through their efforts. We also had an election for Tennessee State officers while there. The Tennessee troops voted for Judge Robert L. Caruthers for Governor and for their respective Congressmen in their districts. The State Department was at Chattanooga at that time, and we suppose that the returns of the election were made to them. We have never seen any published returns of the election, but suppose it held. We suppose it was the only election ever held that had no graft or liquor dispensed as an inducement—truly a prohibition affair.

By the time we were ordered to move, Wheeler's Corps was in splendid condition, both men and horses. Rumors were pending of a great battle, and all were anxious to be off to the war again. Early in September, 1863, we were ordered to the front. At La Fayette, Ga., we met a portion of General Bragg's infantry. He had remained quietly at Chattanooga until the enemy made their appearance in front of the city, when he retreated south; and, marching back to La Fayette, he surprised the enemy, when General Rosecrans hastened to get his scattered army together to give battle. General Thomas, with his large corps, had crossed the Tennessee River at Bridgeport, marching across Sand Mountain toward Rome, Ga., and was separated some distance from General Rosecrans. Our brigade was sent back to Tryon Factory with the infantry brigade of General Helm to meet a Federal command, which we did. After some sharp fighting they retreated with a view of joining the main column of Rosecrans. We continued on their trail, after several hard contests with them, notably at Bluebird Gap and other places, till General Thomas had taken position in McElmore's Cove, when General Bragg made his dispositions to capture them. General Hindman's Division was ordered to a gap in the mountain to prevent Thomas's escape; but for some reason he did not reach it in time to prevent it, and Thomas hurried to join with General Rosecrans. This failure on the part of General Hindman to get to the designated point in time is said to have brought about an inquiry of court-martial. It was evident that but for this failure we would have captured General Thomas's splendid corps. General Wheeler continued his skirmishing with the right wing of General Rosecrans's army till we reached the field of Chickamauga on the evening of the 19th of December.

We relieved General Breckenridge's Division at Glass Mill, on the Chickamauga, where they had had a considerable battle with the enemy under General Negley. Other parts of General Bragg's line on his right had been hotly engaged during the day and late in the evening by the combined attack of Generals Claiborne and Cheatham. Some success had been obtained by them.

I here insert a paper prepared by me after a visit to the battle field of Chickamauga more than twenty years afterwards, and which I was invited to read before Donelson Bivouac and an assemblage of the Daughters of the Confederacy in their hall at Gallatin:

The battle of Chickamauga was fought on Saturday and Sunday, September 19 and 20, 1863, the farthest extremity of the field being about thirteen miles southwest of Chattanooga, extending up to about seven miles of that city, which is about the dividing line between the States of Georgia and Tennessee.

General Rosecrans was in command of the Federal forces, and General Bragg was in command of the Confederates.

We are standing to-day on the exact spot in the old field near Glass Mill where we dismounted to fight, and from which we advanced to take part in that bloody and hard-fought battle between American soldiers. We feel that we are standing upon consecrated ground, baptized as it has been by the best and purest blood that ever pulsated in human veins. It was here, amid the smoke of battle, that the forms of personal friends and comrades faded from our sight and we beheld them no more. As we gaze up into the blue skies that panoply these mountains and valleys, we seem to feel that their spirits hover around here yet, and that we can again commune with them. As imagination paints, we feel that same inspiring emotion which nothing on earth can excite save the busy preparation for battle. As we listen to its roar—the boom of cannon, the crash of musketry, the shouts of advancing columns—we experience the light, airy feeling, twitching of the nerves, and restless expectation that an impending conflict alone can produce, and feel that we breathe an atmosphere high above this earth.

Rosecrans in advancing from Chattanooga had marched by his right flank toward the Alabama line. He had supposed that General Bragg was retreating; and when Bragg marched back, taking position at La Fayette, Ga., he seemingly became alarmed and, with a view of getting together his scattered columns, marched back toward Chattanooga along the line of Missionary Ridge, covered by the mountainous country and the Chickamauga River south of his line of march. About ten days before the battle Wharton's Division of cavalry, to which he belonged, was ordered up from Rome, Ga., where we had been since our retreat from Middle Tennessee. This inactivity had become tiresome, and the order to move was received with delight. The air was pregnant with rumors. A great battle was said to be imminent. The men moved with alacrity and determination, for they felt that the opportunity was at hand when they could

Fourth Tennessee Cavalry Regiment.   25

regain lost territory and drive the enemy beyond their homes. Some scouting and skirmishing took place before the general engagement. We remember that at Tryon Factory, Bluebird Gap, McLemore's Cove, and other places we had hard fighting, driving in their right flank. General Forrest with his cavalry had opened the fight at Reed's Bridge, on the Chickamauga, on Friday, the 18th. On Saturday, the 19th, most of the Confederate army had passed to the north side of the river and confronted the enemy, whose right wing rested at Lee & Gordon's mill and extended in a northern direction, covering the roads leading from La Fayette to Chattanooga. Fighting took place during the day, and late in the evening, by a united charge by Cleburne's and Cheatham's Divisions, they drove the enemy and gained some advantage, but with considerable loss. General Longstreet arrived late that evening, and a portion of his corps came upon the field that night—to wit, McLaws's and Hood's small divisions, numbering not exceeding eight thousand muskets. This was the only portion of his corps that participated in the next day's battle. On consultation that night at Bragg's headquarters, the Confederate army was divided into two wings, General Polk to command the right and General Longstreet the left. The order was for Polk to commence the fight on the morrow at daylight, when it was to be taken up successively along the line to the left. For some cause the attack did not commence until late in the day, which circumstance did and has since caused serious comment regarding the result. We thought then and see now that if the Confederates had had two more hours of daylight General Thomas would have shared the fate of McCook and Crittenden, commanding the other two corps of the enemy, and would have been completely shattered and broken to pieces. This failure of the brave old Bishop to come to time was afterwards the subject of court-martial investigation, though no one ever doubted his courage or loyalty to the cause for which he afterwards gave his life; yet history will hold him responsible for the great mistake, whether caused by subordinates or not. It was midday, we suppose, when

General Wharton's Division was dismounted in the old field upon the bank of the Chickamauga at Glass's Mill. They formed the left of Bragg's line of battle, with Hood's Division on our right at Lee & Gordon's mill. We judged from the firing that the line of battle was some five miles in length, and that the battle was raging with desperate fury at this time.

It was Sunday—a calm, clear September day in the mountains of Georgia, amid scenery that Switzerland could not excel in romantic grandeur. The rich green foliage of the mountains served as a background, and from its sides and gorges arose in dense volumes the sulphurous smoke of battle. The fiery wave of battle boiled and surged in its maddening fury during the evening and until nightfall. Commencing on the right, the deafening thunder would roll along the line toward the left, when it would be taken up and swept back to where it started. The sound indicated with accuracy the result in different parts of the field; for as a column would advance to the charge you would first hear the rapid and quick discharge of the batteries, indicating that their position was threatened, then would come a crash of musketry as if every tree in the forest had fallen, and high above all this the shouts of the Confederates. For a moment a deathlike silence would ensue just there, unmistakably evidencing the fact that the battery had been taken or driven from the field. This would hardly die away at a given point before it would be repeated successively along the line and echoed back again, swelling at times to such a mighty chorus manufactured from the thunders of war that it seemed that both heaven and earth would be torn asunder. Truly

> "Such a din was there,
> As if men fought on earth below
> And fiends in upper air."

We feel our inability to give more than a faint conception of the grandeur of the scene that met the eyes and fell upon the ears of those who participated in the battle of Chickamauga. They can never cease to remember it. The roar of the four hundred cannon from Round Top and Cemetery Hill, at

Fourth Tennessee Cavalry Regiment. 27

Gettysburg, which preceded Pickett's charge, has never been equaled, though the casualties resulting from this grand artillery duel were comparatively few; while at Chickamauga all day long on Sunday there was a series of infantry charges upon batteries in chosen position, in which whole companies and regiments were swept away like the morning mist before the rays of the sun.

While sitting upon our horses listening to all this, we noticed a courier gallop up to General Wharton and deliver a message. We were ordered to dismount, as heretofore stated, and advance toward a battery that was shelling us from an eminence across the Chickamauga and about one-half mile distant. The order to advance was received with lusty cheers, for the men were chafing to go forward. The brigade was composed of the Eighth and Eleventh Texas, the First Kentucky, and the Fourth Tennessee Regiments. Col. Thomas Harrison, of the Eighth Texas, commanded the brigade as senior officer, and Lieut. Col. Paul Anderson was in command of the Fourth Tennessee, which was on the right of the brigade. We moved in column down the road leading to the river and, fording the stream near the mill, formed a line of battle in regular infantry style in the edge of low, level beech woods, and, placing our skirmishers a short distance in front, advanced through the woods. The enemy knew that we were coming and kept up an incessant shelling of the woods, some of our men being injured by limbs of trees torn off by the cannon balls. We had advanced but a short distance when the skirmishers became hotly engaged, which was the signal for a rapid advance, and we swept through the woods, driving the enemy before us. They rallied at a fence at the edge of the woodland, delivered an effective volley, and fell back across a little field to a new line behind a fence and on the edge of another woodland along an eminence where their artillery was planted. As our line emerged from the wood into the open space this battery, shotted with grape, and the line behind the fence, armed with seven-shooting Spencer rifles, opened on us, and a perfect hailstorm of deadly missiles filled the air.

28   Fourth Tennessee Cavalry Regiment.

Being commanded to lie down, we did so for a few moments, and then arose and charged across the field. Just here we sustained our heaviest loss, and in a few moments the Fourth Tennessee had forty men shot down as we arose from the ground. As we rushed across the field the line sustaining the battery broke; and as they ran off many were killed and wounded, two or three hundred of them surrendering in a body. We were struck here with the gallantry of a Federal officer. He was on horseback and with drawn saber was attempting to hold his men to their position. He was killed, and his body fell into our hands. Papers upon his person indicated that he was colonel of the First Ohio Regiment. We went half a mile farther until we drove them beyond Crawfish Springs, the field hospital of the Federal army. This explained, what we could not understand at the time, why we were making a fight so far from the line of our infantry. The Federals had been driven from the line of the Chickamauga, and, this being the only water accessible to them, they had made Crawfish Springs their field hospital. We have learned since that we were fighting the division of Gen. George Crook. Both sides lost quite a number in killed and wounded. Where a stand had been made they were thick upon the ground. The line of attack for a mile was well defined; but, really, though we gained the fight and drove them from the field, our loss in killed and wounded was as great as theirs. The immense crowd of men, tents, vehicles, etc., at Crawfish Springs caused us to believe at first that we had captured the whole Federal army. Dead men in rail pens for protection and wounded men in large circus tents were scattered about over acres of ground, with the accustomed retinue of hospital assistants and not a few shirkers from the fight. This spring is one of the largest and purest of clear water I have ever seen. Its volume is large enough to supply a great city, and the stream that flows from it is that of a small river. After detailing a guard to hold the captives, the remainder of the command were marched back to their horses. The road was full of our ambulances, litters, etc.,

Fourth Tennessee Cavalry Regiment. 29

bearing off the dead and wounded. Here was presented that other phase of grim-visaged war, sickening to look upon: friends and comrades dead and dying who a few hours before were full of life and soldierly enthusiasm; men with their pale, ashy countenances turned toward the sky. Such scenes dissipate the excitement that the advance creates. A friend who was mortally wounded recognized me as we passed. As he evidently wished to say something to me, I stopped and took his cold, icy hand. Fixing his glassy eyes upon me, he said in a faltering voice: "Let my people at home know that I died like a true soldier." He died that night; and his body rests somewhere upon the field his valor helped to win, though his name will never appear in the "count of the battle." His was the fate of thousands of gallant spirits whose memory lives in the hearts of a small circle of acquaintances, but whose heroism has made their commanders great in song and story.

I have had a desire to visit these scenes ever since the war closed. Soldiers are rushed upon battle fields and rushed away, leaving a desire to visit them again. It was just twenty-four years ago and the same hour of the day when I last saw this field where Harrison's Brigade made their fight, yet many things are true to the impressions left; and what a rush of buried memories are resurrected! The old mill where we crossed the Chickamauga looks the same. The woodman's ax has leveled the dense beech grove on the north side through which we moved to the attack. A few scattering trees are still standing to indicate the character of timber that once stood upon the ground. Now it is an inclosed field, upon which is growing in rich luxuriance "the tall yellow corn." I tried to follow the line of our advance, and suppose I did so from the fact that, the timber being cleared away, the high ground upon which the enemy's battery was located is plainly to be seen. I fancied that I found the little hillock on the far edge of the woodland where we were ordered to lie down while the enemy's shot sprinkled us with gravel. I cut a cornstalk from the spot where so many of our men were shot down, and have it yet as a memento. The low log house on Snodgrass Hill is still standing, and looks as it did then. It was here that we captured so many cannons. This point in the field is upon its southern extremity, situated between the road leading from La Fayette and the one leading from Crawfish Springs to Chattanooga. Just here the hardest fighting occurred. The field is still an immense rugged and woody forest, and no particular marks can be seen except now and then the tall stump of a tree. All through the woods for miles the bodies of the trees have been chopped by curio hunters. In a dense jungle at the foot of Snodgrass Hill I noticed a number of graves. The letters on the rotted boards indicated that they were Alabamians. The Dyer, Vittitoe, Glenn, and Ross houses have been preserved, and look as they did then. But after traveling over the field for hours, I might say with truth that there is nothing here to tell the stranger of the spot where one of the bloodiest battles in the world's history was fought. Hundreds of brave men of both armies were buried here in their blankets, and hardly a sign seems to mark their resting place. But the name and fame of Chickamauga will live in history as long as Lookout lifts its rocky ribs to the skies or the river of death winds its way to the sea. As I stood there musing I could not but ask myself the questions: Where are the men who were actors in this bloody drama a quarter of a century ago? Where is the spirit that pervaded this immense host and drove them to deeds of blood and slaughter? The glory, pomp, and circumstance of war have departed, and to such as survived that field and the long years that have passed since then it seems as a shadowy dream, without the semblance of reality.

But to resume: On Sunday night we slept upon the field near General Longstreet's headquarters, at the foot of Snodgrass Hill. At an early hour the Fourth Tennessee was ordered to report to him for orders. We then anticipated a renewal of the battle. He sent us forward toward Chattanooga to report the whereabouts of the enemy. I remember that we passed a little white house near the Chattanooga

Fourth Tennessee Cavalry Regiment.   31

Road. As we approached it, I noticed a hog running through the woods with a soldier's amputated leg in its mouth. This was one of our field hospitals, the window of which was some three or four feet from the ground. The surgeons within as they amputated a limb would throw it out of the window. The pile outside was so high that they would have to brush away the topmost limbs. Just beyond here was an elevated plateau where a hard struggle had taken place. As many as six batteries of the enemy had been broken to pieces. Horses were piled thick one upon the other, mangled and torn in every conceivable shape. Behind these batteries was a long line of Federals who had been killed where they lay. The fence had caught fire, and many of the bodies were burned into a dark crisp. Every tree and bush was marked by balls, and in some places large trees were torn to pieces. To see it, you would conclude that a small bird could not have survived the storm of bullets that swept like a cyclone through the forest.

I have seen paintings depicting the horrors of the battle field which I supposed were overdrawn; but this idea was dispelled at Chickamauga, and I appreciate now the fact that the imagination cannot always do it justice. All through the woods were telegraph wires thrown over the top of the bushes, connecting every part of the Federal line. These were incased in something resembling a cotton rope. Our men utilized them for bridle reins. Everywhere we found abandoned property and gathered up many prisoners—indicating not only a defeat, but a rout of the enemy. We sent back couriers all day long with this information, but no pursuit was made. We went forward on Missionary Ridge as far as Rossville and in sight of Chattanooga, where great consternation existed among the enemy. We were informed that some of them were escaping to the north side of the Tennessee River. On Tuesday, the 22d, with the remainder of General Wheeler's Cavalry Corps, we came through McFarland's Gap and skirmished with the enemy close up to the corporate limits of Chattanooga. We captured their signal flag on the point of Lookout. Its operator worked his machine until hands were laid upon him. We skirmished all day, losing some men in killed and wounded. In the evening we were withdrawn, and here ended the battle of Chickamauga.

The humblest soldier believes we could easily have captured the Federal army on Monday, the 21st of September. The superior valor of the Confederate soldier was again published to the world, but the full measure which soldierly courage had won at fearful cost was permitted to slip away. I fully concur in the comment made by a gallant Federal officer, in speaking of Chickamauga the other day, that "it was the bravest standing-up fight of the Civil War." It has never been depicted as have been the battle fields of Virginia; but no field save Gettysburg, where the forces engaged were larger, can show such a list of killed and wounded as lay upon that field on Sunday night after the battle. The best-authenticated reports from both sides place the killed and wounded alone at 34,000. General Bragg had about 55,000 men, and General Rosecrans had about 65,000 or 70,000. The great battle of Waterloo did not reach this *per centum* by one-half. The Confederates captured 8,000 or 10,000 (not including their wounded), 51 pieces or artillery, 15,000 stands of arms, a large amount of ordinance stores and camp equipage. The enemy were driven from every portion of the field, leaving it in possession of the Confederates. It was fought on ground of their own choosing. In some parts they had erected breastwork protection that had to be assailed by Confederates, frequently in exposed fields; but they were driven from every inch of the field, leaving their killed and wounded in our possession. The Confederate loss in killed and wounded amounted to 17,300, and the Federal loss in killed and wounded 16,800—this for the reason that the Confederates, being the attacking party, were, of course, the more exposed.

Northern writers and speakers sometimes claim that the Confederate army was numerically larger at Chickamauga than the Federal army. I suppose this arises from the fact that they think General Longstreet was there with his entire corps of more than 20,000, when, in fact, but two reduced divisions

Fourth Tennessee Cavalry Regiment. 33

of his corps were there to take part in the battle—namely, Hood's and McLaws's Divisions—and they participated only in the last day's battle. These two divisions did not exceed 8,000. Bragg retreated to Chattanooga from Middle Tennessee a few months before with about 35,000, and the only accessions he had to his army were Quarles's Brigade, from Mobile, numbering 3,000, Hood's and McLaws's Divisions, and a few loose detachments he had collected up from his department. His entire force could not have numbered more than 55,000.

These writers grow very eloquent over Missionary Ridge and draw gorgeous pictures of the "battle above the clouds." The two fields are contiguous, and the battles were fought within a few weeks of each other. They do not admit of a comparison. I would not rob the Federal soldier of a single laurel, but what are the facts? After the battle of Chickamauga, Longstreet had left, taking with him General Bushrod Johnson's Division of the Army of Tennessee, and other troops had returned to their stations; and General Bragg was holding Missionary Ridge with a force not exceeding 25,000 men, who were clamoring for a change of commanders. What could they now promise themselves with a smaller army against a heavily reënforced enemy? All of the renowned Federal leaders were at Missionary Ridge—Grant, Sherman, Hooker, Sheridan, and others—with an army of over 100,000. With such numerical strength and the prestige of such commanders it was possible, as it proved, to break through our thin line at a given point and, taking it in reverse, to drive the Confederates from their position. But here was committed a graver error than Bragg had made at Chickamauga, for the Confederate army should have been captured. Instead of a vigorous onset and pursuit, but a feeble one was made, and that was arrested by a single division under Pat Cleburne at Ringgold Gap, a few miles below there.

Chickamauga and Gettysburg were the two great battles of the war, the one in the Middle West and the other in the East. They were the pivotal fields upon which the cause of the South turned. Two more hours of daylight at Chickamauga on Sunday, and an assault by General Lee at Gettysburg with his entire army, would have brought about a different result. On these two occasions the Confederate had reached the zenith of his strength and enthusiasm. After this he was too intelligent not to know that we was wasting his weakening strength beating against a mighty stone which gathered force as it moved. He fought bravely and with some degree of success until the last, but with the desperation of a forlorn hope.

We cannot conclude without saying a word to the ladies who have honored this occasion with their presence. In fact, any meeting of Confederate soldiers would be incomplete without your presence. I would not be extravagant in what I say; but in truth the Southern woman has been the truest, the best, and the most devoted friend the Confederate soldier ever had. During the war she was his ministering angel in the camp, on the march, and in the hospital. She has been the light and sunshine of the desolated home that the war left him. Her sweet words of cheer have smoothed the rugged pathway of life and have guided his footsteps toward prosperity again. Her devotion has never flagged nor faltered for a moment; and to-day she is at work aiding and assisting the old, disabled, and indigent soldier, making happy his declining years. How can we forget you? We should be untrue to every principle of gratitude to do so. Before I die I want to see some lasting testimonial given expressive of our appreciation. Were I permitted to name it, it would be a shaft of the purest marble, the tall summit of which would touch the skies, and I would plant it upon the highest point of old Lookout, in full view of Chickamauga's ensanguined field, where so many of the sons of Tennessee gave their lives for what is *just* and *right.*

CHAPTER III.

WHEELER'S RAID INTO MIDDLE TENNESSEE IN 1863.

IN the latter part of September, 1863, just after the battle of Chickamauga, by order of General Bragg, General Wheeler was sent into Middle Tennessee with his cavalry corps. The Army of Tennessee was occupying the field they had so gallantly won at Chickamauga. He moved up the Cleveland Road to Red Clay, and forded the Tennessee River at or near Cottonport, some thirty miles above Chattanooga. The object of the raid was to cut off all supplies from the North for Rosecrans's army, then at Chattanooga. The Nashville and Chattanooga Railroad from Bridgeport to Chattanooga was then in possession of the Confederates. The opposite bank of the Tennessee was closely picketed by the enemy, and the command was to keep as still as possible so as not to draw their attention until we had crossed. We reached the ford after a night's ride, and rested there till daylight. I can never forget the beauty and picturesqueness of the scene that was presented that moonlight night, when four or five thousand cavalry forded the beautiful Tennessee. It happened that the Fourth Tennessee Regiment was in front; and, headed by a single guide, we descended the banks and dropped into the river, and then the line swung down the stream across the silvery surface of the broad waters, like the windings of a huge dark serpent. When we reached the opposite shore, I looked back upon the scene presented. This, with the reflection that we had turned our faces homeward again after our glorious victory, was soul-inspiring indeed. Nearly half a century has elapsed, but its recollection is as vivid in my memory as it was then. No creation of art could have been more imposing. There is too much stern reality in a soldier's life for such to claim his attention, but this scene has left an impression that I can never forget.

As we reached the opposite shore the gray dawn of a bright September morning was breaking upon us. About one-half of the regiment was dismounted and silently moved up the bank. But a few moments had elapsed before the bang of a solitary gun was heard, and in another second bang! bang! bang! went the guns, and then a perfect fusillade. All were now wide awake, and the stillness of the scene was suddenly transformed into busy preparation for a fight. Another regiment was hurried forward, and thundered down the road leading from the river in the direction of the firing. A few more shots were heard, and all was still again. A large picket of mounted men had been driven off with the loss of several men and some prisoners. The remainder of the command moved out from the river as they came over, and in due time all were safely over. The trail of the ford was a devious one and very deep in places. One would reasonably suppose that many mishaps would have occurred, but nothing of a serious character happened.

The command then moved toward Middle Tennessee across the mountains into the Sequatchie Valley, where we went into camp for the night at the crossroads. Nothing of note occurred during the day. About daylight the following morning we were aroused by an order to saddle up and mount our horses, as the bugle sounded "boots and saddles." In a few moments more we were moving down the valley at a rapid rate, not knowing at the time what was up. How vividly these stirring scenes flit across my memory! And how many incidents of dash and spirit do they bring to mind of the early morning "racket, when from out the empty saddlebows bravely they fell"! A few miles away we commenced overhauling Federal wagons, partially plundered; then the cry of a wagon train was raised. As the pace quickened, these captures thickened along the way; and after going ten or twelve miles down the valley to the vicinity of Jasper, there opened the richest scene that the eye of a cavalryman can behold. Along the side of the mountain hundreds of large Federal wagons were standing, with their big white covers on them, like so many African elephants, solemn in their stately grandeur. They had been rushed up there by the teamsters and abandoned. This was too rich a bonanza to be left without an escort; and in a few moments the rifles sounded from the mountain sides, indicating that we would have to do some fighting for such booty. Men were dismounted in haste and hurried to the right and left. A vigorous fire was kept up for a while, when the enemy, seeing that they were greatly outnumbered, surrendered after some casualties on both sides. The escort numbered 1,200, with many drivers of the wagons. Some of them had escaped by cutting loose the mules and mounting them. We knew that there was a large infantry force not many miles away, and we set to work destroying everything at once. Orders were given that no plunder was to be carried off. This, however, was but partially enforced. The wagons were loaded with all manner of clothing and rations for the army of General Rosecrans. Among the wagons were a number belonging to sutlers, with rich stores of all kinds. The result of the capture was seven hundred and fifty wagons, twenty-six hundred fat mules, and twelve hundred prisoners. The wagons, or the most of them, were loaded with rations for the army. The enemy were afraid to risk railroad transportation, and were endeavoring to provision their army at Chattanooga by means of wagons from McMinnville. It had rained the night before and left the roads so slippery that the wagons could not go over the steep mountain pass. Such of the mules as we could not take off were destroyed. The wagons and the greater part of their contents were destroyed on the spot, the débris covering acres of ground. I was particularly struck with the fine harness that had been stripped from the mules, as it lay chin-deep over ten acres of ground. Such a calamity as this would have been most seriously felt by us, and would have retarded movements for months; but with "Uncle Sam," with all the world at his back, it made no perceptible difference. If it created a ripple of discomfort anywhere, we never had the satisfaction of knowing it.

From here we moved on toward McMinnville, traveling all night long with the prisoners, mules, and a few of the wagons. General Dibrell had been sent forward from the crossroads where we camped to take McMinnville. We reached there the next morning. Dibrell had captured the garrison of four hundred, with stores that had been shipped there by rail to be transported by wagon train to Chattanooga. It was said that there was a full suit of clothing for every soldier in Rosecrans's army, besides an immense amount of rations. During the night we overtook the guard in charge of the prisoners on foot. As we passed them I noticed a boy among them who could not have been over ten or twelve years of age, dressed in full Federal uniform. I asked him what he was doing there, and he answered that he was a soldier and a marker for a Michigan regiment. I took him up behind me and carried him the remainder of the night, leaving him with the guard in charge of other prisoners captured at McMinnville. We now had about sixteen hundred prisoners on our hands, and the most perilous part of our raid was still before us. So it was concluded that we would parole them. Marching them out a few miles from McMinnville, we ordered them to hold up their right hands, swearing not to take up arms again until they were legally exchanged, and then started them toward the Kentucky line. How many of them observed their parole, we will never know; but it seemed to us then and afterwards that for every one we killed or captured half a dozen would rise up in their places. When we lost a man, he was "dead for certain," and, worse still, none was to be had to stand in his place. In fact, it was this that forced us to quit fighting after four years, during which time we had the satisfaction of knowing that we were giving them about all they could stand up to, and this after calling to their aid the negroes and an immense foreign importation.

From McMinnville General Wheeler moved toward Murfreesboro. The column was a very long and cumbersome one with the mules and wagons we were attempting to take with us. We must have been close on the rear of the column, for by the time we reached Woodbury (one-half of the distance) we were in a gallop; and when we reached Murfreesboro we were at running speed. We found the command in line of battle close up to the town, forming a semicircle covering the roads leading to the south. We took position in line, and remained there probably half the day, expecting every moment to be ordered to charge the town. All at once we moved in column down the Shelbyville Pike. The object was then comprehended to be a feint to cover the passing of the led stock and wagons. During the halt here miles of railroad track was destroyed. Christiana is a station on the Chattanooga Railroad where a ludicrous little episode transpired *en passant*. The pike was about half a mile from the station, but in sight. A body of bluecoats were seen about the station, and a small troop was sent over to take them in. After approaching the place, something like a cannon was observed upon an eminence back of the station, with the gunners standing about it ready to fire. The information was sent back to the pike, and one of Lieutenant White's guns was brought down. About the time it was placed in position to rake the station half a dozen white handkerchiefs were flaunted in the air. We went over to receive the surrender, and the would-be artillery was found to be an ordinary stovepipe set on a couple of wagon wheels. There was a set of about one hundred jolly, well-fed fellows, belonging to an Indiana regiment. They were well fixed up and were equipped with every paraphernalia for camp life—in fact, they had more plunder about them than a brigade of our army. Of this, what was not appropriated was destroyed, with apologies, however, to our newly made friends, whom we paroled and started back toward Murfreesboro. Many detours of this kind were made from the main column during the raid, and hundreds of prisoners were taken and much property was destroyed.

At Shelbyville we expected to make a fight, as it was reported that a considerable force of the enemy was there and were prepared for us. On approaching the place the next morning, we found they had evacuated the town. Before leaving they had torn down the courthouse on the Square, and with the débris blocked all the streets leading to it. Had they held their ground, certainly some blood would have been spilled before taking the place. We found a great many shops, sutler's stores, etc., in the town, well supplied with goods of every description. These were owned by the Northern camp followers, who failed to get sufficient warning for their removal. Such plunder was considered as legitimate for capture as a United States mule or wagon, and to many it was much more acceptable. No Southern sympathizer would be granted this privilege. Commanding officers would attempt to restrain in a degree, but efforts were generally futile; and the result was that, after a raiding party had left a place,

Fourth Tennessee Cavalry Regiment. 43

not much was left to commence business on again. Both armies pleaded alike to this charge. I noticed soldiers moving out of town with their horses heavily laden with some articles that you would imagine were the last things they would have need of. A couple of ladies had come to town that morning to make some purchases. When they saw what had happened, they waved their handkerchiefs and cheered lustily for Jeff Davis. The soldiers gathered around them, filled their buggy full of goods, and then escorted them out of the town.

From here the command moved out near the Lewisburg and Nashville Pike and went into camp. I think we remained there as long as two days. It is said that General Wheeler's object was to await the return of scouting parties. We had created such a stir among the enemy that they took the time to set on our trail all the forces that were available. It seemed that it should have been the policy of the commanding general to have hastened our escape at this time, as the men, I am sorry to say, were so full of plunder that fighting had gone out of their minds, and they were anxious to get to a safe place where they could make an inventory of their property. However, we moved out one morning toward Lewisburg. The Fourth Tennessee and the First Kentucky Regiments were the rear guard. The first intimation that we had of the presence of the enemy was when cannon balls came crashing through the timber and we could hear the firing of our men and the enemy out on the pike, half a mile off. We sent Captain Wyly, of the Fourth Tennessee, down in that direction. He returned in a few moments, reporting that the enemy were between us and the remainder of the command. Lieut. Col. Paul Anderson and Colonel Chenyworth, of the First Kentucky, held a hasty consultation, when it was concluded that we would cut our way through. When this was announced, it was amusing to see the men falling out of their new Yankee uniforms and donning the faded gray again. It was more amusing still, as I think of it, when the gallant Colonel Chenyworth waved his sword over his head and took his position in front of his regiment, crying out in a loud voice, "Follow me, my brave Kentuckians!" as we moved down a blind pathway overhung with bushes. The two regiments had hardly gotten straightened out when bang! bang! went the enemy's guns, seemingly only a few paces distant in the dense growth. The order was given, "Right into line"; and we moved through the woods one hundred yards or more, when we could see to our left a narrow lane leading out to the pike, and could see our men engaged fighting the enemy. Then the order was given, "Left into column," as we made for the lane. Fortunately, this lane was old and well-worn, and the roadway dipped considerably. By drooping on their horses' necks, this, with the fence, afforded protection to the men from the firing of the enemy, about a hundred yards across a little field. The two regiments went through with but few casualties, and joined with the remainder of the command in the fight. When I meet an old comrade who was present, he always asks: "Did you ever see as much kindling wood flying in the air as at that time?" Here opened up what is well remembered as the battle of Farmington. I wish I were prepared with the data to give a correct account of this fight, but I am unable from memory to give more than the results. I think both sides lost about equally in killed and wounded—say, about two hundred each. We fought for two hours, when General Wheeler learned that a large column of the enemy both in our rear and on the right flank was moving to surround us. The Confederates quietly and without pursuit moved off down the pike toward Lewisburg. The enemy afterwards picked up and made prisoners about one hundred of our men who had not joined the column when the fight took place. Among the number of Confederates captured at the battle of Farmington was the present well-known and efficient Secretary of the State Pension Board, Capt. John P. Hickman. He and his squad had been on detail duty, and were endeavoring to get to their company when captured. He was probably the youngest man in his company. He was confined in Rock Island Prison, and was not released until some weeks after the surrender of the armies. General Wharton, Colonel Cook, Major Christian, Captain Jarmin, and Capt. Polk Blackburn were among the wounded. Blackburn was very seriously wounded, and was thereby rendered incapable of further service during the war. He is now living at Lynnville, Giles County, Tenn., as one of the best-known and most worthy citizens of the county. He has represented that county several times in the State Legislature. The enemy ought to have destroyed us at Farmington. The Confederates were flushed with booty, and the Federals were smarting under their heavy losses in men and material.

We camped at Cornersville that night, along the road. It was quite cold, and the men had to burn (what the owner doubtless thought afterwards) a considerable amount of rails. The next day we passed through Pulaski. Here the Fourth Tennessee was detailed to hold till sundown the bridge that spans Richland Creek. The remainder of the command passed on toward the ford at Bainbridge, on the Tennessee River. We sat upon our horses that evening and watched for hours long lines of Federals as they came over the hills into the town, and expected every moment for them to open upon us. We were commanded to hold the bridge at all hazards—in fact, to be sacrificed, if need be, for the good of the cause. All of which would have read very heroically to the boys of the fourth reader of the next generation, but it was void of sentiment to us as we watched with supreme satisfaction the god of day sink behind the western horizon. Never had we seen so lovely a sunset. We ventured five minutes longer at the post, and then followed the command. We traveled all night and overtook the rear guard a few miles from the river the next morning. It consisted of about two hundred and fifty men, a remnant of Gen. John Morgan's command after his capture in Indiana. They were in command of that gallant soldier Capt. J. D. Kirkpatrick, whom we knew well; and to many of the men we expressed our fear of their capture, as we knew that the enemy had been convinced of our intention and were now pressing us vigorously with a heavy force. We passed on to the river, which we forded without interruption, near Bainbridge, Ala. Our conjectures about Captain Kirkpatrick proved too true, for we learned afterwards from those who escaped that the enemy rushed upon them from every point of the compass, frenzied that we should escape so successfully. About one-half of the men were killed or wounded and captured, not, however, without having inflicted severe loss upon their assailants.

Thus ended Wheeler's celebrated raid in 1863, commencing at the crossing of the Tennessee River at Cottonport, above Chattanooga, and ending with the crossing of the Tennessee River at Bainbridge, Ala.—about four weeks' time in passing from crossing to crossing. The result was as follows: We killed, wounded, and captured of the enemy three thousand men; burned and brought out one thousand wagons; captured thirty-five hundred mules and horses, half of which I suppose we had to abandon in the fight at Farmington. I cannot estimate the loss of the enemy in stores of clothing, provisions, arms and ammunition, the destruction of miles of railroad tracks, bridges, engines, etc., but it was immense. Our own loss in men, from all causes, was eleven hundred, which loss was replaced to a great extent by new recruits and absentees we brought out with us.

CHAPTER IV.

IN EAST TENNESSEE.

WE remained a short time in the vicinity of Bainbridge, Ala., getting horses shod, etc. Many soldiers who had been cut off while in Tennessee crossed the river at different points and rejoined their command. In rejoining the Army of Tennessee we again passed through the field of the battle of Chickamauga. Though it had been six weeks since we had seen it, much of the ravages of the battle were still to be seen. I regret to say that many of the bodies of the Federal soldiers were lying where they fell, but such is the state of war. Missionary Ridge extended from Rossville Gap to a point above Chattanooga where the Chickamauga River empties into the Tennessee River, and about four miles from the city. General Bragg was occupying its top, a distance of four or five miles in length, with his thin line of about twenty-five thousand muskets. From its summit the immense army of General Grant could be seen in the vicinity of Chattanooga. It was naturally a very strong position, and no army near the number of the Confederates could have driven them from it.

The Fourth Tennessee was ordered from here to Trenton, Ga., for the purpose of picketing the gaps in Lookout Mountain, notably at Johnson's Crook and other places some twenty miles from Chattanooga and on the extreme left. I suppose they were sent out there from the fact that a good many members of Company H lived at Bridgeport, Ala., and were familiar with the country and railroad track from there to Chattanooga. These same men had been detailed by order of General Bragg, and had given him important information preceding the battle of Chickamauga. They had been highly complimented by General Bragg on their scouts and the information they had given him. On reaching Trenton, Lieut. Col. Paul F. Anderson availed himself of the first opportunity he had had of making his report to brigade headquarters of the action the regiment had taken in the battle of Chickamauga. The same appears in the war records published by the United States government after the war. When Richmond fell the Federals captured many of the records of the Confederate government that were on file at the Capitol. We have copied it verbatim:

HEADQUARTERS FOURTH TENNESSEE CAVALRY REGIMENT,
In Field, Trenton, Ga., October 30, 1863.

Capt. W. B. Sayers, Adjutant General Harrison's Brigade, Wharton's Division, Wheeler's Corps.

Sir: The report of the action taken by this regiment in the battle of Chickamauga has been delayed by reason of the fact that immediately after the battle we were ordered to Middle Tennessee with the balance of Wheeler's Corps and did not return from that most eventful raid until a few days ago. On or about the 10th of September, 1863, we received while at

Fourth Tennessee Cavalry Regiment. 51

Rome, Ga., marching orders from the commanding general, and reported to him near La Fayette, Ga., where our infantry were being mobilized. A corps of the enemy had crossed the Tennessee River at Bridgeport, Ala., and, crossing Sand Mountain, marched toward Rome. We were sent to the front, and were engaged in daily skirmishing till the battle occurred. On the 15th of September, in conjunction with Gen. Ben Harden Helm's brigade of infantry, at Tryon Factory, on the Rome Road, we had quite a brush with the enemy, driving them off; also at Catlett's Gap, Bluebird Gap, McLemore's Cove, and other places, driving them toward Chattanooga to the right wing of Rosecrans's army. On Saturday evening, September 19, Wharton's division of cavalry relieved Gen. John C. Breckenridge's infantry division at Glass's Mill, on the south bank of the Chickamauga River. He had had a heavy fight there that evening with General Negley's Federal division, and still farther to the right there had been heavy fighting. We remained in this position during the night, ascertaining that about the time Breckenridge was moved to the right Negley's infantry had moved to the Federal left, Gen. George Crook's cavalry taking Negley's position at Glass's Mill. At an early hour on Sunday morning, September 20, the skirmishers from both armies faced each other along the banks of the Chickamauga. About eleven o'clock the enemy planted a battery upon an eminence half a mile distant and commenced vigorously to shell us. At this time the battle to our right was raging with desperate fury along the whole line, and seemed to be a succession of infantry charges upon batteries in chosen position. You would first hear the rapid discharges of the guns, indicating that their position was threatened. Then would come the crash of musketry, as if every tree in the forest had fallen, and, high above all this, the shouts of the Confederates. We could tell unmistakably that we were driving them. It was twelve o'clock in the day, we suppose, when General Wharton ordered the brigade to dismount and take the battery that was shelling us from across the Chickamauga. The brigade consisted of the Eighth and Eleventh Texas, the First Kentucky, and the Fourth Tennessee, Col. Thomas Harrison commanding. The Eighth Texas remained mounted, while the other regiments counted off (No. 4 being directed to hold the horses) and formed line in infantry style. We forded the river at the mill, formed line in the edge of a low beech wood, placed our skirmishers in front, and advanced through the woods. The enemy knew we were coming, and kept shelling the woods. Some of our men were injured by the limbs of trees torn off by cannon balls. We had advanced but a short distance before the skirmishers became hotly engaged, which was the signal for a rapid advance, and we swept through the woods, driving the enemy before us. They rallied at a fence at the outer edge of the woods. After delivering an effective volley at us, they fell back rapidly across a small field to the position of their battery on the hill. As we emerged from the woods, this battery, shotted with grape and the support armed with sevenshooting Spencer rifles, opened upon us. We were commanded to lie down, which we did for a moment, then arose and charged across the field. The battery limbered up and disappeared. We killed many of the enemy as they ran off. About two hundred surrendered in a body. We pursued for some distance till we came in sight of Crawfish Springs, and were the first to reach that place, where we captured an immense host. Besides their killed and wounded, the enemy lost a large number of wagons, hospital attendants, and many shirkers from the fight. When we first came in sight, we supposed that the whole army had surrendered to us, so large was the crowd that met our sight. Our loss was considerable. The line of attack for a mile or more was well defined with the killed and wounded, and where a stand was made they lay thick upon the ground. This was our first experience with the seven-shooting Spencer rifle. We armed two of our companies from the captures. We do not think the enemy's loss in killed or wounded exceeded our own. However, we captured several hundred prisoners on the field. Among the killed was Capt. J. J. Partin, of Company L. Lieutenants

Fourth Tennessee Cavalry Regiment. 53

Barbee, Corbett, Preston, Scruggs, and McLean were among the wounded. The regiment's loss in killed and wounded was forty-five, the details of which from the company officers accompanies this report.

After the capture of Crawfish Springs, we left a guard there. Being ordered to our horses, we mounted and moved rapidly to Lee and Gordon's Mill, where we crossed the bridge and, charging down the road, captured a long line of prisoners, wagons, ambulances, etc. We bivouacked upon the field of battle Sunday night, and at an early hour on Monday morning the regiment was ordered to report to General Longstreet, which we did. He ordered us forward toward Chattanooga, and all day long we were sending him couriers, telling him that the enemy had retreated into Chattanooga, leaving behind every evidence of a complete rout and defeat. We secured many prisoners and much abandoned property. On Tuesday, September 22, with the balance of Wheeler's cavalry, we skirmished with the enemy up to the line of the corporate limits of Chattanooga. We captured the signal flag of the enemy on the point of Lookout Mountain. The officer worked his machine until hands were laid upon him. This ended the battle of Chickamauga, and we left the field on Wednesday, the 23d, with the balance of Wheeler's cavalry on the raid into Middle Tennessee.

Permit me to say that I never found my regiment in better fighting trim. From the highest ranking officer to the humblest private they seemed to vie with each other in the performance of a soldier's duty. Where all demeaned themselves with such soldierly fidelity it would be invidious to make individual mention, but I must be permitted to mention the following: Surgeon W. T. Delaney, who was often in the thickest of the battle caring for the dead and wounded, and his assistant, Dr. T. A. Allen. Captain Grissim, Quartermaster, and Capt. R. O. McLean, Commissary, both rendered efficient service upon the field and in attending to the wants of the men. I would like to mention acts of individual courage of men and officers, but time forbids. A grateful country will remember them and embalm their names as heroes worthy of honor and distinction.

I am respectfully, PAUL F. ANDERSON,
Lieutenant Colonel Commanding Fourth Tennessee Cavalry.
GEORGE B. GUILD,
Adjutant.

The Regiment remained in the vicinity of Trenton, and were not ordered back to the main army till after the battles of Lookout Mountain, Orchard Knob, and Missionary Ridge had been fought, including the battle of Ringgold, which occurred successively from the 23d to the 27th of November, 1863.

Gen. Joe Hooker's Corps bravely led the assault up Lookout Mountain. They were gallantly resisted by General Walthall's brave little brigade of less than one thousand Confederates. General Hooker's men reached the Cravens house, which stands there still, and is, I suppose, three-fourths of the distance from the base and one-half the altitude of the mountain. Some distance from there the palisades of solid rock rise to the summit of the mountain, a distance of several hundred feet, very precipitately. The enemy halted at the Cravens house for the night. The next morning, everything appearing to be so quiet, a call was made for volunteers to go up and view the situation. A captain and twelve men from a Kentucky regiment went up and reported the fact that a citizen had informed them that "they had left the night before." This ended the "Battle above the Clouds." Lookout Mountain and Orchard Knob were both outposts of the army on Missionary Ridge, with small commands at each.

The Confederates were driven from Orchard Knob the next day, and on the third day General Grant assaulted Missionary Ridge with his whole army, attacking the entire line of General Bragg. At some points the line held out bravely, repulsing every assault, and were about to conclude that they had successfully repulsed General Grant's large army. But at last he penetrated the left of General Bragg's line, pouring in in large force and, taking the line in reverse, drove the Confederates in rout and confusion from the summit, capturing a large number of prisoners, many of whom, we regret to say, abandoned their colors by voluntarily surrendering to the enemy. No pursuit was made; if there had been, one-half of General Bragg's force would have been captured. At a favorable position near Ringgold, Ga., Gen. Pat Cleburne placed his division and artillery to await the coming of the enemy. He killed and wounded twenty-five hundred of them, with comparatively little loss of his own. The enemy withdrew and did not attempt to come any farther. The Confederates fell back to Dalton, Ga., and Wheeler's Cavalry Corps were left on outpost duty at Tunnel Hill, about seven miles north of Dalton.

On the point of Lookout Mountain, near the magnificent monument erected by the State of New York, are quite a number of tablets which were agreed upon and placed there by a joint committee of ex-Federal and ex-Confederate soldiers, with the following inscription upon their faces:

> In the battle of Chattanooga, from November 23 to November 27, 1863, which includes Orchard Knob, Lookout Mountain, Missionary Ridge, and Ringgold Gap, Ga., it is authoritatively written that the Confederates had eight divisions and the Federals thirteen.

It must be remembered that the Confederate divisions were much smaller than the Federals'. The enemy had been recruited to the highest point, while the Confederates from long service had but little to draw upon and were very small. The Confederates in these four battles, from November 23 to November 27, lost in killed, wounded, and missing 6,667; the Federal loss in killed and wounded alone was 5,824. The Confederates missing were 4,146; the Federals, comparatively nothing. We know the fact that nearly all the missing from the Confederate ranks were men who voluntarily left their ranks in the rout at Missionary Ridge. The loss of the two armies in killed and wounded, then, was as follows: Federals, 5,824; Confederates, 2,521. The Federal loss in killed and wounded was more than double that of the Confederates in the four engagements.

CHAPTER V.

CAMPAIGNING IN GEORGIA.

AFTER the Army of Tennessee had become settled in their winter quarters at Dalton, Ga., in December, 1863, criticism of General Bragg became hot and severe both on the part of the soldiers and the citizens, and a change of commander was demanded of the government; so much so that General Bragg tendered his resignation, and General Joseph E. Johnston was appointed in his stead.

General Braxton Bragg was seemingly a cold, austere officer and a thorough disciplinarian, but no one ever doubted his bravery and patriotism. The greatest battles fought by the Army of Tennessee were fought while he was commander in chief. His plans and orders for battle could not be excelled in their clocklike accuracy. Every soldier knew that when Bragg got ready to fight it was to be a real fight, and some one was sure to be hurt before it was over. He was particularly unfortunate in the failure of his officers in obeying important orders. He died without giving to the public a history of his campaigns, as other generals have done. But we must add that Bragg seemed to lose his head at the supreme moment after gaining a battle and let its fruits slip out of his grasp when he could have accomplished decisive results, as was the case at Murfreesboro and Chickamauga. He was a great favorite with President Davis, and was given a position in the War Department at Richmond. Just before the war closed he was placed in the field again. He fought a battle at Kingston, N. C., defeating General Cox and capturing fifteen hundred prisoners and some field artillery. Let us forget his faults and remember with pride his valor as a soldier and his patriotism to his native Southland.

Gen. Joseph E. Johnston's appointment to the chief command of the Army of Tennessee was received with much satisfaction by the soldiers. The morale of the army had depreciated after the battle of Chickamauga, and especially after the disastrous rout at Missionary Ridge. The transportation facilities of the army—horses, mules, wagons, etc.—were in bad condition. The ranks had greatly diminished in numbers, and there was no expectation of their being recruited except from conscript camps and the return of absentees. The Confederate armies at Gettysburg and Chickamauga on the two occasions had reached the zenith of their strength and enthusiasm. General Johnston, upon assuming command, soon exhibited his great ability as an organizer, in which he had no superior; and it was but a little while till all of his departments put on a cheery appearance, and, what is better, the morale of his soldiers showed confidence and enthusiasm again. Men and horses were well supplied with good, substantial rations—not dainty food, for it could not be had. Drills of men and officers were held daily, and dress parades were the order of the day. He showed, too, that he was in every sense a thorough disciplinarian. We thought General Bragg was well up in the service in this regard, but General Johnston far excelled him. In the maximum punishment meted out to deserters judge advocates were kept busy. We remember on one occasion to have met Col. Andrew Ewing in the road near Tunnel Hill. While we were talking a volley of musketry was heard from the direction of the infantry encampment at Dalton, when he remarked that the volley had killed twelve deserters. Colonel Ewing was a distinguished lawyer, whose home was at Nashville, and was then Judge-Advocate-General of the army. Notwithstanding this, General Johnston was popular with the soldiers and had their fullest confidence.

General Wheeler's headquarters were at Tunnel Hill, some seven miles from Dalton. His cavalry were kept busy all winter in scouting and fighting back the enemy. Some of his encounters approached the dignity of a battle, in which he lost in killed and wounded a good many men and inflicted a like loss upon the enemy. The country surrounding Tunnel Hill and Dalton was thin, mountainous land and very poor in production and sparse in population. The subsistence of the army had to be brought there by railway. The soldiers always say that they went hungry longer there than at any other encampment during the war. However, I don't think any one really suffered.

General Sherman did not begin his march on Atlanta till the 1st of May, 1864. (See Appendix, C.) His army was more than double in number that of General Johnston, and he had all the reserves he could ask for, which he received time and time again before reaching Atlanta. General Johnston had no accessions but, as has been stated, from conscript camps and absentees, except the brigade of General Quarles, from Mobile, and probably some few small detachments of infantry and cavalry from other points in the South that joined during the march to Atlanta.

The Fourth Tennessee Cavalry happened to be holding the advance station in front of Tunnel Hill and on a direct line to Chattanooga when Sherman commenced his march, giving and receiving the first shots that were fired. The cavalry contested every foot of ground to the vicinity of Dalton, having quite a battle on the outskirts of the town. It was ascertained from scouts that Sherman, about the time he began his advance on Tunnel Hill, had sent a large column of his army to the right to flank Dalton. General Johnston had anticipated this movement, and had a strong line of works at Resaca, about fourteen miles below, to which he hastened with his little army. Thus Sherman began what

Fourth Tennessee Cavalry Regiment. 61

his large force enabled him to do: while he would attack in front with a formidable force, he would use as large a one for flanking purposes against his enemy's rear. When Sherman came up, a heavy battle took place at Resaca, lasting two days, and in which both sides lost a large number in killed and wounded. It was here that Col. S. S. Stanton, of the Tennessee infantry, was killed. It is not designed in this brief narrative to undertake to describe specifically these battles, and the reader can consult the battle reports. Among others, see the history that General Johnston has contributed of his campaigns to the Southern war lore. We know, however, that Sherman's losses at Resaca were heavier than the Confederates'; for we fought behind breastworks most of the time, which protected us to some extent. About the second or third day at Resaca, Johnston was forced to fall back to Kingston (or Calhoun), where the Federals were crossing the river. In fact, the Atlanta campaign of Sherman was a series of flank movements upon General Johnston's army. He would approach his front with a large army and send a like column to the rear to break his communications. The Federal army was driven off at Kingston. The next halt of Johnston's was near Cassville, Ga., where he issued his well-remembered battle order to the effect that "we would now turn upon the enemy and give battle." This order, as it was read to the different commands, was received with the wildest enthusiasm. The bright reflection from the long lines of the enemy's guns across the open space was an inspiration for the troops to move upon them at once. Some delay ensued, when General Johnston was informed by a staff officer from General Hood that the enemy could enfilade his lines, and that he would not be able to hold it. This from one of his highest ranking officers caused him to countermand the order, to the great dissatisfaction of the troops. That night Johnston retired, and it was not surprising that some soldiers dropped out of line, to be picked up by the enemy.

About Allatoona we had some fighting, participated in by detachments of the army. From here General Wheeler was sent back across the river to protect and drive off a force that was destroying some large manufacturing establishments. In the fight that ensued he killed and wounded quite a number of the enemy and destroyed some two hundred wagons. We had some more heavy skirmishing with the enemy at Allatoona; then we were hastened to New Hope, some distance to the right rear, to meet the enemy. On arriving there, the Fourth Tennessee, in conjunction with a brigade of A. P. Stewart's infantry, had a hard fight, but finally drove the enemy back. The regiment had quite a number of killed and wounded. That evening General Stewart built some temporary breastworks. At night (about ten o'clock, I suppose) a large force of the enemy attacked Stewart's works, but were repulsed with heavy loss. It is stated that seven hundred and fifty soldiers were found dead in front of General Granberry's line, and that many of the Federal attacking column were in an intoxicated condition and actually staggered over the works when they were captured. At another time General Bate's division made an attack upon the enemy protected by breastworks, but was repulsed with heavy loss. There was hard fighting on other portions of the line during our three or four days of battle at New Hope Church, but no general engagement of the army took place.

We left there on a dark, rainy night, going to Marietta. The infantry had preceded us, leaving the cavalry in the ditches; later we followed, leaving about ten o'clock at night. It had been raining, and the road which the infantry had passed over was left much torn up. I remember that a cavalryman just ahead of us went down in a mudhole, horse and rider; and as he scrambled to his feet again, he cried out to the amusement of the boys: "Be aisy, men; old Joe will get them yet." This was the most comforting expression we heard during the long, dark ride through the slush and mud.

General Johnston fell back to Kennesaw Mountain, and the enemy, coming up, assaulted the position with a large force. "Fighting Joe" Hooker again led the attacking force of the enemy. Gen. Frank Cheatham's division held the center of the Confederate line, where the most desperate part of the fighting took place, though other portions were hotly engaged. It was a brave attack made by the enemy. Some of them came up to the works, and many of them were killed near our line. The battle lasted several hours before the enemy were repulsed. The next day Sherman asked an armistice to bury his dead, which was granted. General Johnston in his report of the battle says that "the Federal loss was 4,000 or 5,000. More of Sherman's best soldiers lay dead and wounded than the number of British veterans that fell in General Jackson's celebrated battle at New Orleans."

In the vicinity of Kennesaw stands Lone, or Pine, Mountain, somewhat isolated and standing to itself. Lieutenant General Polk had occupied its base with a force in temporary breastworks—to wit, with General Bate's division. He had gone over with his staff to make observations of the enemy, as it afforded a fine view of the surrounding country. The position of his infantry was a constant target for the enemy's largest guns. On reaching the summit, Polk and his staff dismounted and, walking out to the front, were plainly seen by the gunners, who immediately commenced a furious cannonade, and about the first shot killed General Polk. His death was greatly lamented by the whole army. He was educated at West Point, but had retired from the army to become a minister of the gospel; and when he enlisted in the Confederate army he was a bishop in the Episcopal Church. Since the beginning of the war he had served most gallantly in the Confederate army as a general in the Army of Tennessee. He had taken a conspicuous part in all of its campaigns and battles. Gen. A. P. Stewart was made lieutenant general in his place, Lieutenant General Hardee having before this been transferred to another department. John B. Hood and A. P. Stewart became lieutenant generals of the Army of Tennessee.

Several hot contests were had with the enemy in the neighborhood of Marietta, amounting frequently to the dignity of a battle. In some of these we remember that Col. Ed Cook, of the Thirty-Second Tennessee, Colonel Walker, of the Third Tennessee, and his adjutant, John Douglas, were among the number killed.

Marietta, Ga., is a distance of some twenty miles from Atlanta, the Chattahoochee River intervening eight or ten miles from the latter city. Its banks are low and approachable, and the river is fordable in many places. Further than the usual cannonading and skirmishing of the two armies, nothing of interest occurred until General Johnston reached Atlanta. General Johnston fought battles out at Peachtree Creek and perhaps at other places. In one of these Colonel Walker, of the Nineteenth Tennessee Infantry, was killed. He was the father of Laps Walker, the well-known and able editor of the Chattanooga *Times*. Colonel Walker was in command of the brigade when killed. It was well known in the army at this time that General Johnston was making ready to attack Sherman by placing the militia under command of General Smith in the forts and fortifications around Atlanta, and then moving with his entire army to the flank of Sherman, to defeat him and destroy his army before they could reach their base at Chattanooga. The army was in high spirits in anticipation of this movement. Instead of being dispirited by the long retrograde movements, their confidence had increased, and they were ready to obey his every order with supreme confidence in its success.

At this time President Davis visited the army at Atlanta, and in a few days General Johnston was relieved of the command of the Army of Tennessee and Lieut. Gen. J. B. Hood named as his successor. It is said that another had been asked to take the command, but had declined, saying that the army had the supremest confidence in General Johnston. I repeat what was reported and generally believed. Nothing could have overwhelmed both soldiers and citizens with more surprise than this order. Soldiers were speechless, shaking their heads in answer to questions, as much as to say that a great mistake had been made, predicting the most direful results, which were proved in so brief a time afterwards. I remember having heard an able address since the war from that highly intellectual Christian gentleman and splendid soldier, Lieut. Gen. A. P. Stewart, upon this subject. His position in the army and in its councils enabled him to speak advisedly and in stronger and more convincing words than I have used.

The distance from Dalton to Atlanta is about seventy-five miles. The contending armies were seventy days in covering the distance—a little more than a mile a day. It was a great battle scene from its beginning to its close. At night the camp fires of the two armies were visible one from the other. A number of large battles were fought, and many were killed and wounded on both sides. The daytime was an incessant crash of musketry from the skirmishers and heavy cannonading from batteries. In fact, from the number of killed and wounded in many of these skirmishes, they would be called battles at the present time. There was no evidence of rout or hasty retreat on the part of the Confederates along the way, not even the waste of a peck of corn meal.

I notice the statement made in a magazine recently that in looking over the private papers of Mr. Davis there was found a correspondence between him and his Secretary of War, Mr. Benjamin, when the following reasons were assigned for the dismissal of General Johnston: "That he had failed to give battle to the enemy at the many available positions passed from Dalton to Atlanta, and that he now proposed to move upon the enemy with his entire army, leaving the State militia to hold the works at Atlanta." It has been said, and General Johnston repeats it in his book styled "Johnston's Narrative of His Campaigns," that "his loss from Dalton to Atlanta was ten thousand, while that of the enemy was equal to the number of the soldiers then in his army." I take this to mean at least thirty-five thousand. Sherman was enabled to keep his army up to its original strength by troops sent him from time to time during the campaign. The Confederates had none except those I have mentioned before. General Hood in taking command issued a battle order, and in ten days' time is said to have lost as many men as Johnston had during the campaign.

CHAPTER VI.

GENERAL WHEELER'S CAPTURE OF THE COMMANDS
OF GENERALS MCCOOK AND STONEMAN.

ON the 27th of July, 1864, General Hood ordered Wheeler's cavalry to the rear of Atlanta with a view of beating off a Federal raid commanded by Generals McCook and Stoneman, having for its purpose the breaking up of Southern communications, releasing the large army of Federal prisoners at Andersonville, destroying manufactories, etc. Before leaving Atlanta General Wheeler divided his cavalry of about five thousand into two columns, Generals Dibrell and Iverson going to the left after General Stoneman, and assuming in person the command of the column to the right sent after General McCook. Wheeler came up with McCook at Jonesboro, thirty miles below Atlanta, where his troops were engaged in destroying the railroad tracks. The Confederates at once charged them. After a short but spirited fight, they drove them off with some loss in killed, wounded, and prisoners. McCook retreated toward Newnan, Ga. He was hotly pursued all night long. At a bridge, just at daylight, we came up with a large picket of the enemy. We at once charged them and drove them off. The entire command hastened over the bridge and in a little while came up with the enemy. A battle ensued in which there was a considerable loss on both sides.

After a little while the enemy resumed their retreat toward Newnan, hotly pursued by the Confederates. We here discovered that they had been looting and burning our wagon trains, which we had not seen since we left Dalton, and which had been sent south three months before. McCook, on approaching Newnan, had been fired upon by a militia command stationed at the depot, which caused him to turn to the left and take position in a hilly and wooded locality near the town, awaiting the coming of the Confederates. The Confederates arrived in a little while, though in a somewhat disordered and straggling way, after two days and a night of hard and strenuous riding and fighting. As they came up, without general orders they went into the battle where the fight was raging hottest. The battle, I suppose, lasted two hours. At one time the enemy captured the line of dismounted horses of the Fourth Tennessee Regiment, when the Regiment wheeled about and recaptured them, killing, wounding, and taking prisoners. The Regiment lost quite a number here. Among the killed was James Turner, orderly sergeant of Company A. J. A. Stewart lost his right arm. Both were good soldiers and most excellent gentlemen. Fighting took place in several places on the field. A white flag was displayed, and General McCook and about fifteen hundred of his men surrendered with a battery of artillery; also about three hundred of our soldiers who were with the train were recaptured, among them being a soldier wearing the military coat of Capt. W. W. Thompson (the only brother of my wife), of the Fourteenth Tennessee Infantry, who was killed at Chancellorsville, Va. I had it in a box in our wagons that had been destroyed by the enemy, and the soldier had put it on with a view of saving it for me, which I greatly appreciated, for I was anxious to return it to his father and mother. Besides the fifteen hundred taken as prisoners, some five hundred of General McCook's men escaped during the parley. They were pursued to the river, which they crossed after abandoning most of their horses. Some of the men threw away their arms and accouterments to lighten their bodies, it was supposed, for swimming the river. As we passed through Newnan on our return to the Army of Tennessee, the hospital on the streets was crowded to overflowing with wounded soldiers.

Generals Dibrell and Iverson were equally as successful in their engagement with Stoneman near Milledgeville, Ga., capturing him and his entire command. McCook and Stoneman, when their commands joined, were to make a joint attack upon the prison at Andersonville.

After this Wheeler's Corps was ordered to rendezvous at Covington, Ga., to the left of Atlanta. He had destroyed the entire cavalry force of Sherman. He remained at Covington some days recuperating and having horses shod, when he was ordered upon his second raid into Middle Tennessee. He moved to the rear of Sherman at Atlanta, and, going north along the railroad, destroyed miles of track, depots, and bridges, and capturing some small detachments, with but little resistance until he reached Dalton. Here the enemy had built a strong fortress well supplied with cannon, and had a considerable force to defend the place. A line of battle was formed as if we were going to charge, and by a feint its strength was developed. It was wisely concluded that the booty was not worth the cost of capture. However, we succeeded in destroying a large lot of provisions that had accumulated there and a large camp of wagons, tents, etc., located in the suburbs of the town, which were abandoned by the occupants, who, we supposed, had taken refuge in the fort. Some of these occupants must have been quartermasters, for an enterprising soldier picked up a tin box that contained several thousand dollars in greenbacks.

From here we moved to the right, and, entering East Tennessee, we crossed the railroad at Strawberry Plains, sixteen miles above Knoxville. Here a cavalry force coming up from Knoxville attacked our rear; but upon turning on them, they were put to flight and were pursued to the outskirts of the city, killing and wounding some, capturing prisoners and horses, with the loss of a few of our men in killed and wounded.

After this Wheeler moved over into Sequatchie Valley, where the Fourth Tennessee was detached and sent to Tracy City with a view of capturing a force that was said to be occupying an unfinished fort. Upon reaching the place, Lieut. Col. Paul Anderson made his disposition for capture by detailing Lieut. W. H. Phillips, of Company F, with ten men to charge down the road leading to the fort in order to attract their attention, when Colonel Anderson would come up from the rear, where the fort was said to be unfinished and open, and capture it. Before reaching his position, Colonel Anderson discovered that the opening had been closed and that there were as many of the enemy on the inside of the log structure as he had on the outside. He at once dispatched a message to Lieutenant Phillips countermanding the order; but before it was delivered Phillips, growing impatient, charged as directed. The courier reached there in time to see Phillips upon the ground in front of the fort shooting at the portholes, and saw him scramble to his feet and stagger across the road into the timber where his comrades had sought protection. He had been terribly wounded in the breast and shoulder, showing evidence of paralysis from the wounds. A conveyance was impressed with a view of taking him and others who had been wounded with us; but after traveling a mile or two, Phillips was suffering so that he asked to be left at a house to die. His friends thought that he certainly could live but a little while. For six months after this he was reported in company reports as killed in action in Tennessee. To the surprise of every one, and just before the surrender, Phillips came marching into camp, very thin and feeble, but alive. He said that after he had been at the house a few days the Federals found him there; and when he was able to be moved, they carried him to the fort and had every attention paid to him, saying he was too brave a man to die from neglect. Phillips remained at the fort for some time. When he had convalesced sufficiently, a proposition was made to him that if he wanted to go home to his family he could do so if he would take the oath. This he declined to do, and asked to be sent north as a prisoner. He was sent to Johnson's Island Prison. Being a very much disabled prisoner, he was sent on exchange to Richmond in March, 1865, reaching the camp of his regiment a few days before the battle of Bentonville. He died a few years ago a highly respected citizen, but never recovered from his severe wounds and suffered the remainder of his life.

The Fourth Tennessee Cavalry left Tracy City for Lebanon with a view of overtaking General Wheeler. A great many of our soldiers were permitted to go by their homes to remount themselves, pick up absentees, and obtain recruits if possible. I availed myself of this opportunity, thinking it was the last chance I would have to visit my family, residing in Gallatin, Tenn., whom I had not seen for nearly three years. An account of this individual raid I made upon Gallatin I here insert under the head

BEHIND THE LINES.

I tell this incident, not so much to interest the present generation, who have lived so close to it and have heard for themselves from the enactors in the War between the States many and probably more hazardous undertakings than here related, but that the future generation may know the state of affairs that existed in this country about the homes of those soldiers who were driven from them and sought to see their families again after a forced exile of years.

Soon after starting from Atlanta on General Wheeler's second raid into Middle Tennessee, in 1864, I resolved to go into Gallatin, my home and native place, and see my family, from whom I had been absent for more than two years. I knew that Gallatin had been occupied by the Federal forces a long time, and that the commandants of the place, Payne and then Scarret, had been placed there for their well-known disposition to lord it over a helpless and noncombatant population. Many outrageous crimes had been committed by them, and

76 *Fourth Tennessee Cavalry Regiment.*

scores of Confederate soldiers had been brutally murdered for no other reason than that they sought to see their dear ones again. The darkest chapter in our War between the States could be written under this head. I was fully posted then of the hazard of such an undertaking; but I wanted to see my wife and little boy (who was but a few weeks old when I left there), and I fully determined in my own mind to risk it, as I felt convinced that this would be the last opportunity.

When the command reached the Sequatchie Valley, General Wheeler sent the Regiment down to Tracy City to take an unfinished fort that was in course of erection and to be occupied by a garrison. Fearing that we would not return in time to make my anticipated trip home, I went to Lieut. Col. Anderson, my warm-hearted and true friend, and told him how disappointed I was, disclosing to him my well-digested plan to go into Gallatin at night, stay concealed in the house all day, and return the next night, making myself unknown to any I should meet along the way. I reminded him that it might be possible to obtain valuable information for the army. The Colonel did not think my plan feasible, remarking in his nasal way: "Guild, you are certain to be killed or captured." I told him that I had resolved to make the attempt and believed I could successfully accomplish it. He finally concluded to let me go.

Capt. Marcellus Grissim, Knot Harris, Billy Bell,

and Clay Smith, Colonel Smith's colored servant, went with me. These men all lived on this side of the Cumberland River and some distance from Gallatin, and I was the only one intending to go that far. We at once set out for Crossville, on the mountain, and then to Cookeville. Soon after leaving the Regiment we found ourselves in the country infested with the bushwhacking band of Tinker Dave Beatty, the notorious Federal jayhawker, a terror to Southern sympathizers in that part of the State, whose whole object was to kill, not to capture. On several occasions as we passed along the citizens would tell us in terrified whispers that he and some of his band had but a moment before preceded us, and death was certain if we fell into his hands, as they took no prisoners. To avoid such results, we concluded to lay by in the daytime at some secluded place and travel at night. Some very amusing things occurred during our night riding. A good many Federal soldiers belonging to Colonel Stokes's regiment were furloughed and at home. If we chanced to meet any of these upon the road, and we sometimes would as we passed houses, we told them we were Federal soldiers and had been sent to notify them to return at once to their post at Carthage, Tenn., as it was rumored that Wheeler was coming across the mountain.

These things delayed the little squad of ours in reaching their destination. Captain Grissim's home was in Smith County, near Rome. Before reaching there I had promised him to stay all night to rest up before I started alone for Gallatin. When I stated that we had been delayed so that I was anxious to start at once in order to get back and meet the command as it passed Lebanon, he still insisted, but I declined. Leaving my horse and Clay, the servant, with him, I started on foot to Gallatin. It was then near sundown. My first object was to get a boatman to paddle me across the river. I found much difficulty in this. I had on all my army equipment—gray uniform, two army pistols around me, and haversack in which I carried all my papers as adjutant of the Regiment. But over these I had on a long linen duster, which somewhat concealed them from view. I had determined, if I was captured, to have no evidence upon me as a spy or to disguise the fact that I was a Confederate soldier, though the old duster would easily conceal me, and I posed as a Federal soldier when asking information. I had walked some distance down the road when I overtook a man driving an ox wagon going in the same direction. I asked him if he knew where I could get some one to put me across the river. He replied that he did not, and wanted to know who I was and where I was going. I told him that I was one of Colonel Stokes's men and had been absent on furlough at my home in the mountains; and that, having heard that the rebels were marching that way,

I was hurrying to get to my command across the river. I noticed him eying me closely, and after a few words more he said to me: "Come, get up on the tongue of the cart. I don't believe you are telling the truth; I have seen you somewhere before. You are no Yankee, but a Confederate soldier. My name is Walton. Tell me what you are after." He spoke so frankly that I concluded at once that he would do to confide in. I got on the cart, told him who I was, and that I wanted to go to Gallatin that night and return the next; that I had left my horse and servant with Captain Grissim, and when I returned we would go over and meet General Wheeler's command as it passed Lebanon. He knew Captain Grissim, but said: "If you go to Gallatin, you will certainly be killed. The meanest kind of an officer is in command there, and he kills every Confederate soldier he captures. Besides, I learned that they are greatly stirred up, are impressing the citizens to work in strengthening the fort, and have drawn in their picket posts close up to the town." This was a worse state of affairs than I had anticipated; still I replied that I would attempt it. At this he said: "If you will go, get up and ride; I live about one mile down the road. Go by the house and get your supper, and I will put you across the river." It was dark when we reached the house, and his wife had prepared supper. After supper I started; and after getting across the river, he gave me directions how to reach the Gallatin and Hartsville Turnpike, about four miles distant.

Unfortunately, after reaching the Sumner County side I remembered the house of a man whom I knew well as a most enthusiastic Southern man and in full sympathy with the Confederate cause when I left there. So I went to see him. He did not seem to know me; and when I told him my name, he still seemed not to recognize me. It was too apparent that two years of Yankee rule had wrought a change, cooling his Southern ardor; and I left him, congratulating myself that I had not told him where I was going. I fully resolved that I would make no more experiments in this direction.

I was now pretty well posted, so I continued my course toward the pike. A short distance from the pike I passed the house of another citizen whom I knew well, Mr. Carey. He was standing at his front gate, and I easily recognized him in the starlight and the candle reflection from his house, which stood near by. I passed, not intending to stop with a "Howdy-do," when he remarked: "You seem to be traveling at a late hour and all alone." "Yes," I replied. "I am anxious to get to my command at Gallatin." He spoke up quickly, remarking: "If you had been here a few minutes ago, you would have met up with scouts that stopped here, fed their horses, and got something to eat." I asked him what direction they went, and he replied: "To Gallatin from Carthage." He then set out and without any questions from me told me the same condition of things that my friend Walton had told me, except that he added that all the roads out of Gallatin were being scouted, as they were anticipating an attack then from Wheeler. About this time he stopped and remarked: "Listen! I can hear the horses' feet upon the pike traveling toward Gallatin." This was a very probable occurrence; but I could not hear them, though I seized the opportunity to start in that direction, saying: "I can probably overtake a straggling cavalryman, and I will get to ride." I congratulated myself again, but with more satisfaction for sharpness than I did in the former interview, and with the fuller determination that this would end my interviewing of citizens and would risk all on the information I had. I am satisfied, however, that if I had confided my case to Mr. Carey he would have assisted me to the utmost extent.

I then began my travel down the pike toward Gallatin, about fourteen miles distant, stopping to listen occasionally. At Bledsoe's Creek, six miles from the town, I stopped on the hill near the tollgate to listen, and thought I heard the sound of horses' hoofs on the turnpike. After waiting awhile, I moved across the bridge and, to avoid meeting any one, got over the fence with a view of traveling parallel with the pike until I came to a lane that led from the pike to Cairo, my intention being when I struck the lane to travel along it back to the pike again. When I reached the lane, I sat on the fence, and to save me I could not remember which end to take. I remember to this day my sitting there and trying to reason it out. I do not think I was asleep; but I was so exhausted from six weeks' riding day and night that I became bewildered and chose the wrong end of the lane. When consciousness returned, I found myself near Cairo, more than a mile off of my route. I immediately turned and retraced my steps to the turnpike. When I reached it, the same bewilderment again overtook me. I stood there for some time debating with myself the way to Gallatin, and at length set out again, supposing I was right until I found myself approaching the point at Bledsoe's Bridge which I had left more than an hour before.

I knew every foot of ground in the neighborhood, and had traveled these roads hundreds of times. My grandfather Blackmore's farm was contiguous to them, and the people in the neighborhood were friends whom I knew and had visited. I had gone at least four miles out of my way; and looking toward the east, I could discover evidences of day breaking. I knew it would be death to be caught in that vicinity in daylight, and, tired, worn-out, and footsore, I struck a trot toward Gallatin with all the vim and strength I could command, determined not again to leave the beaten track. At Mr. Barry's I took the old Cairo Road to Gallatin. At the Chambers farm I left it and, passing Mr. Calgy's place, passed on to my father's farm and house, south of Gallatin, on the Lebanon road and about half a mile from the courthouse at Gallatin. The Hartsville Pike that I traveled down approached Gallatin from the east.

As I got into the field near the house day was evidently breaking in the east. I looked toward town and saw a camp fire on Fitzgerald's Hill, which adjoins the corporation line, and saw soldiers standing around. I knew then that this was the picket base, and that the vidette stand would be near the front gate of the yard that stood upon the next eminence in the road from the picket. The house stood on the opposite side of the road from the direction I was approaching. Thus the whole situation was before me. Concluding that there might be a foot race before the fight was over, I thought that I had better lighten myself for such an event, should it occur. As I have said, I had been carrying two large army pistols in my belt, and they had become burdensome, rubbing the skin on my side and hips till it seemed as if they were pieces of raw beef. So I concluded to conceal one of them in the fence corner and get it when I returned. I did not intend to disarm myself, and I retained one army pistol and a smaller one that I had in my haversack, a Smith & Wesson. A difficulty was the last thing I could wish for, but I wanted to be prepared for any forced defense.

I then proceeded down the fence toward the house, expecting to pass through the hedge of burdock along the pike and on to the opposite side from the house, where I remembered there was an opening covered by rails. On reaching it, I looked up and down the pike and saw the pickets about one hundred yards off, standing at the upper gate of my father's yard fence and looking south, with their backs toward me. All seemed right at the guard post; and then, lifting myself quietly over the rails, I slipped across the road to the garden fence between the guard and vidette stand and, climbing over, fell into the garden. Another lightning process suggested itself to me—to pull off the heavy cavalry boots that I had swapped for with one of General McCook's cavalry soldiers at Newnan, Ga., a few weeks before. They had skinned my feet till I could hardly hobble along. So, going into the summer house, I sat down on a bench and shed them, and never saw them again. I proceeded to the yard and, going around the house, saw a light burning in my mother's room and felt then (which was a fact) that she was up with an invalid sister. I pulled up the back steps to a gallery in the rear, and, going to my mother's room and making a smothered knock at the door, heard some one say: "Who is that?" In a low tone of voice I whispered my name, when I heard my sister exclaim: "Lord, ma, it is Brother George!" The door was opened, and I quietly entered. I could not, if I wanted to, tell what happened then. It was a sudden and unanticipated apparition. Both my mother and sister looked dazed and could not believe for a moment what they saw. If I had fallen from the skies, they could not have been more surprised. After some explanations and conversation, I asked for my wife and baby, and was told that they were on a visit to Nashville. I shall not undertake to describe the deep disappointment that this news created. I remember to have exclaimed in tones of deep despair: "Is it possible, after all, that I will not be permitted to see them?" After a little while my mother said to me: "My son, do you know the risk you are running? The soldiers are at the gate, and every day they are through the yard, and they frequently come into the house. There is not a negro about the place who would not take pleasure in informing them that you are here. The soldiers in town are expecting an attack. They are strengthening the fort in anticipation of this, and are impressing everybody that comes about town to work on the fortifications. Besides, if they capture you, they will kill you and burn up the house." I said: "Yes, I understand all this and know what risk I am running. But if you do as I suggest, I do not think any harm will come of it. I have come to stay but to-day, and will return to the army as soon as it is night again. Let me go upstairs to the room looking toward town. I am so tired that as soon as I strike the bed I will go to sleep, when you can lock the door; and if any of you want to see me, you can slip in during the day, and there is no reason that any one's attention should be directed to the room if you are vigilant and discreet. Let no one know the fact that I am here but those of the immediate family, for I did not come for or expect to see any one else. As soon as it gets quiet after nightfall, I will come downstairs and, after telling you all good-by, will start back to the army."

I had to pass a long and open porch before reaching this room. Daylight was then evident. Looking toward the front gate, the pickets were plainly to be seen, and to shelter myself from their view I got down on my hands and knees and crawled to the door of the room. Without divesting myself of clothing, I fell across the bed, and in a few minutes was fast asleep. If any one came into the room before twelve o'clock in the day, I did not know it. About this hour I heard some one in the room, and, looking up, I discovered that it was my wife. She had left Nashville the evening before, and had come in her buggy as far as Hendersonville, where she stayed all night with an acquaintance, and then went on to her father's house in Gallatin. Her father, Dr. George Thompson, who had been out to see me, had told her that I was at my father's, and without getting out of the buggy she had driven on out. She said, further, that she had heard in Nashville the morning before that Wheeler was on a raid into Middle Tennessee, and that she had started at once that she might be where I could communicate with her if possible. I then asked to see my little boy, when she answered, "No," saying that my mother and herself had concluded that it might reveal the fact to others that I was in the house; that the child was a great pet with the soldiers that came around the house; and that he was constantly telling them that his father had a gun too, and a pistol and sword, and that he was coming home soon and would cut their heads off and shoot them too. I asked if she could not devise some way for me to see him, when she said that she would contrive to get him out on the porch under a side window of the room, which she did, and I had the pleasure in this way of seeing him. At night when I left he was asleep in his bed, and before leaving I gave the little fellow a hug and kissed him farewell.

During the day members of the family would slip in and see me for a few minutes, one at a time. I saw only five people to speak to during my day's visit. My father was at Nashville practicing law. He had to do something to meet the necessities of a large and helpless family. The large farm was in ruins, the stock was all taken, and the servants had gone to the Yankees. My father had been arrested by Andrew Johnson, who was military Governor of Tennessee, as a civil prisoner and sent to Fort Mackinac, Mich. After an incarceration of nearly a year, he was exchanged for Judge Ritter, of Kentucky. Gen. John H. Morgan had arrested Ritter for the purpose of making the exchange.

About four o'clock in the evening I was dozing upon the bed when I heard loud talking. Glancing out of the window, I saw Federal soldiers running through the yard in every direction in an excited way. I at once concluded that they had been informed that I was in the house, and that they were making their arrangements to kill or capture me. I concluded at once to meet it as best I could. I hobbled to a chair and, placing it in the room opposite the door, drew my army pistol, clicked the cylinder around to see that all was right, and, holding it under my coat so that it could not be seen, I awaited the issue. I remained in this state of suspense ten or fifteen minutes, I suppose, when my wife tiptoed into the room to inform me that a citizen of Wilson County had come into Gallatin that day, that the guard was after him to put him to work on the fortifications, that he had evaded them and had run through the large yard full of shrubbery to make his escape, and that everything was now quiet. I do not know that I was ever more relieved by a piece of information.

The five individuals mentioned above continued

to slip in and see me until I left. They were much distressed that I could not take clothing with me, which, of course, I sadly needed. However, they managed to get me a soft pair of shoes to take the place of the army boots that I had abandoned. I do not think I am exaggerating at all when I say that if a corps of army surgeons had made an examination of my person they would have unanimously reported that I would not be able to move in ten days. Between nine and ten o'clock, all being quiet, I got up and adjusted my clothing, haversack, and pistol, and, taking my shoes in my hand, quietly walked down to my mother's room, where I was to meet them before leaving. I quietly unbolted the door and walked in. I shall never forget that scene. It remains in my memory yet as a "death watch." All were weeping with smothered sobbing. There was no occasion to remain longer now, so I immediately commenced bidding them farewell. The last to meet me was my old mother, who as she arose from the old family rocker and threw her arms about my neck said in these never-to-be-forgotten words: "O, my son! Do you not think your little army is already crushed and overwhelmed? I sit here day after day thinking and praying for you all and listening to the running of train after train of soldiers from the North, and feel that you cannot withstand such numbers." I replied: "It is a gloomy outlook, indeed; but my duty as I feel it is to return to my comrades, to share whatever fate may befall them."

At that I stepped out into the dark and began my sad tramp again. Somehow I felt stronger and better in getting out in the open air once more. I concluded that I would go around the pickets this time on their front. I stopped at a convenient stump and put on my shoes for the first time. They were exactly what I needed; they were loose upon my feet and gave me no annoyance. After traveling around, I remembered my other pistol, and went toward the place I had hid it. Upon reaching there, I searched and searched, but could not find it. After passing through a cornfield and at a point where the lands of my father and Mrs. Calgy joined, I noticed the tall weeds growing in the corners of the fence. It was a first-rate hiding place, and was inviting to rest, which I so much needed. The place was about half a mile from my father's house, where I concluded to avail myself of a night's rest and a day also before proceeding. I argued, too, that if I should be captured out there, there would not be such dire results—in other words, they would not interfere with the family. So I crept into the high weeds, and in a few moments was fast asleep.

When I awoke it was late in the day—a calm, crisp September day in 1864. I could hear the Federal forage wagons lumbering along the pike, and the Federals actually came into the field, which was a very large one, and gathered corn. I quietly lay in the weeds and ate the lunch my folks had placed in my haversack, partaking pretty freely of a bottle of blackberry wine, and then smoked my pipe. I recollect while lying there to have heard the thunder of Wheeler's guns away across the Cumberland. When night came on I went back and had no difficulty in finding my pistol. I felt much refreshed after my night and day's rest, but was absolutely perishing with thirst for water. The bottle of wine had produced it, I suppose. I remembered a wet-weather branch on Mrs. Calgy's farm about a mile distant, and I broke for it. It lay just along the way I was to travel. Upon reaching it, I found a pool of muddy water. Kneeling down, I filled my stomach with the vile stuff; but it did not slake my thirst a particle, and smelled and tasted of a hog wallow strong enough to kill one. I filled my empty wine bottle full, and hurried on to the old spring on the Chambers farm, where my father was reared and educated by his uncle, Colonel Conn, who lived another mile distant, but still along my course of travel. Occasionally I would take a sip from the bottle and wash out my mouth, which seemed to do some good; and when I reached the spring, I filled my stomach full of the sweet beverage, which at once did me great good. I had never before come so near perishing for water, and I know now what it means to thirst.

Upon reaching the Hartsville Pike, I determined not to leave it till I reached Anthony's store, where I was to go on to the Cumberland River, determining that if I met Federal scouts I would conceal myself until the squad passed; and then if I chanced to meet a straggler I would unhorse him and, mounting his horse, go at breakneck speed till I reached the point on the river where my good friend Mr. Walton was to come for me at a given signal. Fortunately, I met no one and proceeded on foot till I reached the vicinity of the river a little after daylight.

I found some difficulty in locating the exact place. Looking about, I recognized the house of a lady and gentleman whom I knew well. Having reached the time and place when I could throw off my disguise, I went over to Mr. McMurtry's house. He and his wife were glad to see me. They had a good breakfast prepared, which I partook of very liberally, telling Mr. McMurtry that Mr. Walton had promised to meet me at the river on giving the usual signal. McMurtry seemed to understand this "grapevine" way of doing, and went with me, giving the customary signal himself. A few minutes later Walton came over in his canoe. About the first words he spoke were to tell me that Captain Grissim had been killed by a scout of Federal soldiers from Carthage on the night I had promised to stay with him and rest before going to Gallatin, that Grissim and two young recruits who were to go to the army with him had all been killed in their mother's yard and in her presence, and that if I had consented to stay that night I certainly would have been killed with them. He stated further that later in the day, and after the scouts had left the neighborhood, he had gone up there and was told where he could find my horse and the servant, who were hiding out; that he had brought them down and concealed them; that the country, he understood, was still full of scouting Federal soldiers; and that I must go up to his house and remain quietly till night, when he would go with me to get my horse. Passing over the river, I did as he suggested. At night I mounted my horse and proceeded toward Lebanon, where I expected to meet some of our command. Before leaving I thanked Mr. Walton for his great kindness; and having nothing to give, I reached in my haversack and, taking out the beautiful little Smith & Wesson pistol, I gave it to him to give to his wife with my thanks for her goodness and her ever-to-be-remembered kindness to a stranger under difficulties.

I expected to close the details of this lengthy incident here, though I do not know how I could have said less; but I feel that I should tell one more hazard I encountered before reaching a point of safety, and it is as follows:

More than a year ago an elderly lady came into my office and asked if I was Mr. Guild. I replied that I was. Then she said: "I am the woman you met when you called at my house, three miles from Lebanon, on the Big Spring Road, in the fall of 1864, to inquire if there were any Yankees at Lebanon. It has been more than forty-five years ago. I moved to Texas soon after the war, and this is my first visit to Tennessee since I left. I have heard from you occasionally since through Tennesseeans I chanced to meet from time to time, and I have frequently thought that if I ever returned to Tennessee I would look you up. You remember the circumstances, don't you?" I replied that I could never forget them. She then proceeded to tell in her own way that she saw me down on the road that night, and that I was seeking information. Three Confederate soldiers of Colonel Starnes's regiment were sitting in the hall with me at the time. They had been visiting their homes in the Rome neighborhood, and were there when Captain Grissim and his young brother and nephew were killed by Colonel Stokes's soldiers from Carthage, and were in search of their regiment. The Federal scouts, whom they were dodging in trying to escape, were patrolling that section. "Yes," I said, "I remember to have seen them when they ran through the hallway into the back yard." "Yes," she said, "when you dismounted and started up the walk to the house, they seized their guns to get ready to shoot you, when I jumped up and said: 'Don't shoot! It may be some acquaintance, and I will go down and meet him to find out his business.'

At that they rushed out of the house. When we met, you told me that your name was Guild, that you were a Confederate soldier, and had been to Gallatin for a few days to see your family, and that you were returning to the army again. You then asked what the condition of things was at Lebanon, and if there were Confederate or Federal soldiers about the place. You said that you had come in with Captain Grissim, and that upon returning to the neighborhood of Rome you learned of the killing and had yourself been looking out for Federal scouts. In reply to your question I said that I did not know, had not been there myself or seen any one who had for the last day or so, and that everybody was afraid to go." Thanking her for the information, I returned to my horse and mounted, proceeding toward Lebanon. She remained at my office an hour, I suppose, in interesting conversation. She told me her name, but, I am sorry to say, it has escaped my memory. I saw her no more, and suppose that she returned to Texas after her visit.

On approaching Lebanon, a deathlike stillness prevailed. I could see neither individuals nor lights about the streets or houses. The numerous white houses glistened in the moonlight like a whitened cemetery. I remembered where Mrs. Dolly Anderson McGregor lived. She was the wife of Capt. Andrew McGregor and a sister of Lieutenant Colonel Anderson, of the Fourth Tennessee Cavalry.

She readily informed me that a Georgia command of cavalry had passed down the street toward Nashville about sundown. I concluded that they would stop at the creek about a mile away to water or feed their horses or probably to camp for the night. I hurried in that direction to overtake them. As I approached Seawell Hill, near the residence of Judge Abe Caruthers (now deceased), I came upon a picket. I went forward and told them who I was, and found out that the Georgia battalion had gone into camp for the night. I told them I was so tired that I would lie down at the post and sleep till daylight, when I would go forward and meet the major of their battalion, whom I knew. I took advantage of the opportunity offered to review the very successful campaign I had just finished; and, to be brief, I wisely concluded that the army was the safest refuge in time of civil war, and that if the war were to last a thousand years I would not undertake a campaign "behind the lines" again. There were too many unanticipated difficulties and hairbreadth escapes along the way. The day that I spent at home was one of untold agonies to my family, such as is hardly possible for human nature to endure. I could not and would not impose it upon them again.

CHAPTER VII.

IN TENNESSEE, VIRGINIA, AND HARASSING SHERMAN.

ON reaching Lebanon, I came up with a squadron or more of the Fourth Georgia. They had been sent out on detached duty, and were trying to overtake the command. General Dibrell came in from White County with four or five hundred men, mostly recruits and returning absentees. We learned definitely that General Wheeler had passed over the Nashville, Chattanooga, and St. Louis Railway near Nashville, and that in passing Franklin he had a fight with the enemy and had gone farther south. General Kelly, a well and favorably known officer of his command, and others had been killed. Dibrell assumed command and marched down the Murfreesboro Pike, expecting to cross the railroad near Smyrna, in order that he might hear something of General Wheeler; but being informed here that Gen. "Cerro Gordo" Williams was at Sparta with a command of about fifteen hundred men and he being the ranking officer, General Dibrell concluded that he would go to Sparta and unite with him. There were not more than three hundred guns in Dibrell's little command at that time.

Upon reaching Blackshop, about eight miles from Murfreesboro, we marched over to the Woodbury

Pike, near Readyville, and went into camp for the night on the first high ground from the bridge. We had been informed by a citizen that a few hours before the Seventh Pennsylvania Cavalry Regiment had passed down the pike toward Murfreesboro. Before lying down on the grass for the night a picket was placed at the bridge. At daylight the next morning this Federal regiment came charging into our camp. It is said that they were eleven hundred strong; for they had just returned from the North, where they had been recruited to the highest limit. Many of the Confederates had not arisen from their pallets. A general mix-up fight was had, our men using their navy pistols and outfighting the Yankees with sabers. General Dibrell rallied the men at the other end of the line and gave the enemy a volley which rather staggered them. After some hard fighting, General Dibrell withdrew his men. No pursuit was made, except that their advance guard attacked our rear guard at the bridge this side of Woodbury and were repulsed. Quite a number of men were killed and wounded on both sides. The Federals captured about one hundred of our disarmed men. With their numerical strength and advantage, they should have captured the entire command of General Dibrell.

We then pursued our way to Sparta. We met General Williams at Sparta with his force of about fifteen hundred men. We went from there over to a place called Sinking Cave, where we remained two days, feeding our horses and having them shod. General Williams concluded to return to the army at Atlanta. We passed on through Crossville and up through Upper East Tennessee. Gen. John H. Morgan had just been killed at Greeneville, Tenn., where he was stationed. The circumstances attending this unnecessary murder greatly exasperated the men. After killing him, it is said that a soldier lifted his dead body up on his horse and paraded the streets of Greeneville with it, amid the cheers of the Federal soldiers. Federal bushwhackers were thick along our line of march and occasionally killed some of our men. This, with the killing of General Morgan, caused our men to retaliate, and they were guilty of some outrageous conduct. General Williams tried to stop it, and had three privates and a lieutenant arrested and regularly tried by court-martial. The facts alleged against them were proved to be true, but the court-martial left it to the commanding general, Williams, to fix the penalty, when he ordered the severest punishment to be enforced— death by hanging. As soon as it was known, four members of the court (one refusing to sign) and the Judge Advocate petitioned General Williams to change his order, claiming that the offense was not at all commensurate with the penalty he imposed. This he refused to do, saying that it was necessary to make an example in order to stop it. His orders were executed the next morning.

When in the neighborhood of Rogersville, Tenn., General Williams received an order from General Breckenridge, at Saltville, Va., to hasten there with his command, as General Burbridge was marching on the place with a view of destroying it. This was the chief salt supply for the Southern States. We passed through Bristol and Abingdon, Va., and reached Saltville in the nick of time, for General Giltner, with his brigade, was skirmishing with the Federals when we came upon the field.

General Breckenridge's force at Saltville consisted of Giltner's small brigade of cavalry, some cadets from the Military Institute in Virginia, workmen about the salt works, and the cavalry command of Gen. "Cerro Gordo" Williams, numbering altogether about three thousand men. Burbridge had a well-equipped command that considerably outnumbered the Confederates. The Fourth and Eighth Tennessee were assigned to a position on a somewhat elevated knoll, in rather an advanced position in the line, and received the first onset of the enemy. They were slow in approaching the line, and our men went forward to meet them. The cry was raised that we were fighting negroes. They were the first we had ever met. Many of them were killed and wounded. There was fighting all along the line, continuing for three hours or more, when Burbridge was driven off

Fourth Tennessee Cavalry Regiment. 101

and commenced to retreat. About six hundred on both sides were killed and wounded. This field presented a scene that was never witnessed before. There were more dead men than wounded. We lost some of our best soldiers.

That night we pursued the enemy, passing over the mountain to a gap with the view of cutting them off. They had to travel over a distance of forty miles on a well-built macadamized road. The mountain path to the gap was only twelve miles in length, and the men had to dismount and lead their horses. The night was very dark, and it was hard to discern the path. Occasionally a horse would make a misstep and tumble down the steep mountain side, when you could hear the noise of falling stones for minutes afterwards as they rolled down and down the precipitate mountain side. There was nothing for the soldiers to do but sit down till daylight near the track the column made. We were told afterwards by some of these soldiers that they found their horses miles below where they fell. I have occasionally met an old soldier who was at Saltville, and about the first thing he would speak of would be: "Did you ever experience anything like that dark night ride at Saltville, Va.? And the wonder is that a number of men were not dashed to pieces down the steep mountain side." We reached the gap at daylight. Burbridge's rear guard was passing through, and we killed and wounded a few of them. We asked an old citizen if any one had ever traveled over the pathway before. He replied: "Occasionally I have seen citizens going over it and coming back with a bag of salt on a lead horse, but nobody that I have ever heard of would dare to do so at nighttime. It is a wonder that half of you were not killed."

When General Williams left Sparta for the Army of Tennessee, at Atlanta, all of the independents and bushwhackers in that part of the State went out with him. It got so hot thereabout, and the Federals were swarming so in Tennessee (like bees), that they concluded the better part of valor was to get away. Champ Ferguson, of the one side, and Dave Beatty, of the other, both, I believe, from Fentress County, were the respective leaders. A warfare had been raging in this part of the State and Southern Kentucky since the beginning of the war, and some outrageous murders had been perpetrated upon citizens as well as soldiers. The name of each was a terror to one side or the other. Champ Ferguson and his followers participated actively at Saltville. After the battle was over a Lieutenant Smith, of the Federal army, was left with others wounded. He was taken to Emory and Henry College, which was made a hospital for both armies. When Ferguson heard the fact, he went over there and killed Lieutenant Smith. It was said that Smith had during the war killed a Colonel Hamilton, who was a comrade, neighbor, and personal friend of Ferguson; that Smith had captured Hamilton after a fight between members of the two clans, and had been ordered with a squad of soldiers to take him to headquarters over in Kentucky; but that, after starting with his prisoner and going a short distance, he ordered his men to take Hamilton to the side of the public road, where he was stood up by a tree and shot to death.

A short time after the Confederates had returned from the surrender, in May, 1865, Ferguson, who had surrendered to the Federals, was undergoing trial by court-martial at Nashville. He had been arrested at Saltville, Va., by order of General Williams for the alleged killing of Smith and sent to Richmond, as we understood it, and we saw him no more afterwards. The war terminated a short time after this. I presume in the confusion of things he was permitted to return to his home in Tennessee. I was told that frequent attempts had been made to capture him; but finally, after being advised and on being assured by Federal authority that if he would surrender he would be given the same terms that had been extended to other Confederates, he gave up. After this he was placed on trial by a military court-martial on various charges of murder. Among others was the charge of the murder of Lieutenant Smith at Emory and Henry College, in Virginia. He was convicted and executed by hanging at Nashville. I do not approve of the murder of Lieutenant Smith, nor do I approve of the promises made Ferguson to induce him to surrender; for if half is true that I have heard about Ferguson, he certainly had his grievances.

Before leaving Saltville for the army, General Williams was ordered under arrest and directed to report at the headquarters of the corps to answer the charge of his failure to join General Wheeler while in Middle Tennessee. We moved through Bristol and down to Jonesboro, Tenn., where we turned and passed over the mountains dividing Tennessee and North Carolina to Asheville, thence to Greenville, S. C., thence to Athens, Ga., and across to Atlanta.

General Hood fought battles on the 22d and 28th of July at Atlanta and then at Lovejoy's Station and Jonesboro, Ga. They were large and hotly contested battles, with heavy losses on both sides, but without material effect. He and General Sherman agreed and exchanged what prisoners either had of the other.

After this General Hood began his campaign into Middle Tennessee. General Dibrell was in command of the forces lately commanded by General Williams. He started at once to overtake General Hood; but after about two days' marching we met General Wheeler with his command returning to Atlanta, with instructions to remain there and watch the movements of General Sherman and follow him in whatever direction he might take. Dibrell also returned to Atlanta with Wheeler, making their joint commands about 3,000 cavalry. As soon as he had ascertained that Hood was moving into Middle Tennessee, Sherman began his march to Savannah, Ga. His army was composed of 64,000 infantry, a large artillery corps, and 5,000 cavalry under General Kilpatrick.

The distance from Atlanta to Savannah is about two hundred miles—about the distance that Nashville is from Memphis. Sherman's line of march was along the Savannah River, giving full protection to his left (for it is a large, deep river). Along the river a strip of rich country extends forty miles out into the State of Georgia. The large crops of rice, cotton, corn, and potatoes were ripened and ready to be gathered into houses. No one ever saw a more enchanting country, and the despoiler had never left his track upon the soil before. The section was thickly settled at the time by old men, women, and children, happy in the enjoyment of peace and plenty, with no means of defense, for the men and boys of legal age were all away from home in the army. Sherman marched through a country forty miles in breadth with his great army, with nothing to hinder his burning and pillaging but about 3,000 cavalry, as we have stated. He left it, when he reached Savannah, a long, black, charred waste of country that a bird could hardly have subsisted upon. Sherman spoke from experience and observation when he said: "War is hell."

When Sherman with his large army of over 70,000 marched out of Atlanta, Wheeler's small force of cavalry commenced at once to skirmish with his advance guard, and did so until he reached Savannah, with an occasional battle with Kilpatrick's cavalry, invariably driving him back upon the infantry support and circumscribing as much as possible the pillaging of Sherman's army. It is said that Sherman deliberately prepared for all of this before commencing his march by mounting a considerable number of his infantry upon horseback, under officers and in companies, to do the pillaging and burning, his cavalry protecting and covering their front while so engaged. It certainly was evident that his men were systematically organized beforehand for this purpose.

After a few days' march, Kilpatrick with his cavalry made a dash for Macon, Ga., with the view of destroying the public works of the Confederates, which had been extensively established in that city. Wheeler at once pursued, heading him off at the village of Griswoldville, some seven miles from Macon. A portion of the Georgia militia was occupying the place when we came up; and when Kilpatrick appeared, a fight ensued lasting some hours. The militia fought like veterans, which convinced us that if Johnston had been permitted to place them in the fortifications around Atlanta when he proposed to lead his entire army against Sherman's flank, he would never have been removed; for they would have held the forts and breastworks as a safe retreat for his infantry, had they failed upon the flank of the enemy. After a fight lasting some hours, Kilpatrick was driven off with loss. Wheeler's, as well as the militia's, loss was considerable. I know that the Fourth Tennessee lost a number of their best soldiers. Kilpatrick soon afterwards made a move toward Augusta, presumably for the same purpose as at Macon; but General Wheeler, ever on the alert, headed him off by a night ride and saved the city.

After this we came up with Kilpatrick at Waynesboro, Ga. It was a dense, foggy morning, so much so that you could hardly discern the form of a man fifty feet ahead. We at once attacked them in a large field near the town in a very mixed-up fight, in which we killed and wounded many and took many prisoners, losing quite a number ourselves. In the midst of the battle, with balls whizzing in every direction, I came across a squad of our men who had taken as prisoners four of the enemy. They were threatening to kill them, when I remonstrated and told them to turn them over to the rear guard near by. Just then an officer of higher rank rode up. I appealed to him, telling him that the soldiers proposed killing them. His only reply was: "They know best what to do with them." As I rode off into the fight, I heard the popping of the pistols, and I could see the prisoners tumbling over into the high sage. I had not proceeded far when I noticed this officer reel from his saddle with a shot in his arm. I could not help saying to myself: "I wish it had been your head shot off." It would be proper here to say that many most outrageous transactions were done by the Federals as they passed through Waynesboro, and these were told to the men. It was enough to excite to vengeance; but nothing can excuse the killing of prisoners after capture, as was done in this case.

Later in the day we came upon Kilpatrick at or near Buckhead Church, where he had intrenched his command behind a long line of fence that (we afterwards ascertained) extended from swamp to swamp, covering his entire front. General Wheeler ordered General Dibrell to proceed to the left flank of the enemy and to attack them, saying that the firing of his guns would be a signal for him to charge the line of fence with the remainder of his force. The signal was given by Dibrell, but probably before the exact situation was observed by him, and Wheeler charged with his entire force mounted. In fifteen minutes Wheeler had many of his men killed and wounded, losing more horses than in any battle during the war. Of course this created confusion for a little while when we went over the works, but the enemy had mounted their horses and were making for their infantry force, which was but a short distance off. This was one battle in which there could be no doubt that our loss was greater than that of the enemy. There could be no controversy over this. There was picked up on the field an officer's military cap indicating high rank. It was supposed to be Kilpatrick's, and General Wheeler returned it to him with his compliments.

It would be a difficult undertaking to relate anything like the destruction of property accomplished in the "march to the sea" by Sherman's men. Every rice and grist mill was burned, as well as cotton gins, barns of corn, and fields of potatoes destroyed; and in some instances dwelling houses, if not burned, were stripped of their contents, which were removed or burned. Fine carpets were torn from the floors, and men were permitted to take them for saddle blankets. Provisions of all kinds—hay, corn, etc.— were destroyed. I have seen smokehouses with the meat all appropriated and barrels of molasses poured out on the floor and mixed with salt and ashes to destroy its use. I have seen, time and again, long rows of dead horses numbering from thirty to one hundred and fifty. Upon taking every mule and horse that the citizens had, they would kill their own, not leaving the citizens as much as a half-dead mule. At night you could tell exactly the position of their army by the light of burning houses, and during the day by the black smoke that hung over their line of march. It was as if there had been a great spring cleaning, and the whole atmosphere was thick with it. Sherman's line of march was well defined by cinders and burning débris. In his report of this march he says:

> We consumed the corn and fodder in the region of country thirty miles on each side of a line from Atlanta to Savannah; also the sweet potatoes, hogs, sheep, and poultry, and carried off more than ten thousand horses and mules. I estimate the damage done to the State of Georgia at *one hundred million dollars* at least, twenty millions of which inured to our benefit, and the remainder was just simply waste and destruction.

Henry Grady, then a resident of Atlanta, in his great speech before the New England Society, of New York City, in speaking of General Sherman a few years after the war, said: "You people up here think he is a great general, but down our way we think he is too fond of meddling with fire." The speaker doubtless thought of saying: "Not till the chapter on his march to the sea is eliminated from his record as a soldier and its black and dark criminality is eradicated from the minds and hearts of the Southern people can we agree to this."

The first and greatest object of a general is to crush and destroy all armed opposition to constituted authority. Why, then, was it that Sherman did not turn and follow Hood into Middle Tennessee when he and Thomas, who had a large army at Nashville, could have crushed the little army of General Hood, as it were, between the upper and nether millstones and thus end the war—anyhow in the Middle West? There was nothing of the strategic in the movement. Was it not a wanton and unnecessary destruction of the property of an unarmed and helpless community and the making homeless and breadless the families of old men, women, and children? Will not the student of the truth of history in after years so conclude as he reads with surprise the report of an American general who has had the temerity to confirm the facts under his own signature?

We continued skirmishing with the enemy, circumscribing their burning and pillaging until we reached the vicinity of Savannah. Shifting to the front of Sherman, we reached Savannah before he did. His march was slow, taking about four or five weeks, giving full time to his soldiers for the work they had set out to accomplish. General Hardee was occupying a line of intrenchment in the front, his force consisting of detachments (including seamen, workmen from the public shops, etc.) numbering altogether a few thousand. General Wheeler with his command took position in the outer breastworks. About this time Fort McAllister, on the coast below there, had fallen. A large force of the enemy were marching up to join Sherman, but before they reached there General Hardee very wisely concluded to abandon the place, which he did by crossing the Savannah River into South Carolina,

CHAPTER VIII.

THE SOUTH CAROLINA CAMPAIGN.

GEN. WADE HAMPTON assumed command as chief of cavalry, although General Wheeler retained command of his old corps. The Fourth Tennessee was sent up the east side of the Savannah River to protect the citizens and prevent the destruction of a large number of rice mills. Their first station was at the plantation of Dr. Chisholm, about thirty miles above Savannah, where we remained several days.

The large rice mill immediately on the Savannah River was an immense frame structure, four stories in height, and afforded an unobstructed view of the country on the other side, including Sherman's line of march to Savannah. The smoldering débris of mills from which smoke was ascending could be seen. There were two or three crops of rice in the mill, to which we were told to help ourselves, for the sheaves of rice made fine feed for our horses after placing it in water the night before. While here the enemy made several attempts to cross the river, but were repulsed. After we had been there several days, at nightfall a young soldier rode up to our camp fire with a lady (whom we presumed to be his mother) riding behind him on his horse. The young man said that he had been informed that we had orders to leave that night. When we informed him that we had and expected to leave at daylight the next morning, he and the lady had a consultation and, approaching the camp fire, removed a lighted fagot and, going over to the mill, applied the torch and burned the mill and its contents, which we were told was worth half a million dollars. The only word he spoke afterwards was that they had "concluded to burn it rather than leave that pleasure to the Yankees."

At Aiken, S. C., we had quite a battle with the enemy. We had just reached the place when a large force unexpectedly appeared at the foot of one of their broad and beautiful streets. We charged them at once and drove them back into the suburbs, where we fought for an hour, finally driving them off with loss. We, too, lost a few men, among whom was Jo Rushing, of Company E. He was a relative of our much esteemed and most efficient Sergt. Maj. W. A. Rushing, who remained with his relative till he died a few days afterwards. Our Sergeant Major is still living, as honorable and worthy a citizen as he made a brave and sturdy soldier during the war. He has been the representative of his constituency in the State Legislature.

After reaching the State of South Carolina, it seemed as if the enemy were invading the State from all directions—north, south, east, and west. It was a difficult matter to calculate when and where we would meet the next marching column. We would meet and check them temporarily, when we would be threatened by another. It seemed that the enemy were making an effort to cover every community in the whole State, still exhibiting their propensity to burn and destroy. I remember having seen some correspondence between General Sherman and General Hampton that appeared in some of the local papers. Sherman had sent a note to Hampton informing him that if his men murdered any more of his after they had surrendered he would retaliate by killing a like number of his prisoners. Hampton replied that when his men found the enemy burning the houses of citizens, as they were in the cases referred to by him in his note, when the women of the house were following his soldiers through the rooms, putting out the fire they had thrown upon the beds and other inflammable objects, no orders would restrain them; and to Sherman's threat to retaliate Hampton replied that he would kill two of his soldiers for every one he executed. I heard no more of the correspondence, but must say that the enemy's destruction still continued.

We moved across the State to the eastern shore, where we had frequent skirmishes with the enemy, sometimes with parties who would come ashore from their blockading ships, notably from a point that we called the Summer House. Late in December, 1864, we found ourselves at Grahamville, S. C., about forty miles below Charleston. I remember that we spent Christmas day there. A few days before General Wheeler gave the men permission to go to the coast and get the wagons filled with oysters in the shell, which we did. I suppose that was the first time an army was feasted upon oysters. The soldiers would sit out in the open before a log-heap fire, throw the shells into the fire, toast them sufficiently, then break them open and eat the delicious bivalve. This reminded us of Christmas time before the war, "when life ran high and without a ripple upon its surface to disturb its happiness." It was there that we learned for the first time of General Hood's disastrous campaign into Middle Tennessee.

General Hood marched to Sherman's rear at Atlanta, Ga., and, going north along the railroad, attacked the Federals at Allatoona, Ga., in a well-fortified fortress, with General Cockrell's brigade, who, after a most gallant fight, was repulsed with heavy loss. Hood then deflected to the left and north, reaching the Tennessee River at or near Decatur, Ala. Crossing the river, he moved north, passing through Mt. Pleasant and on to Columbia, Tenn. There, after considerable cannonading and musketry, he flanked the place and, reaching the neighborhood of Spring Hill, stopped for the night. He gave specific orders to attack the enemy if they attempted to move along the pike toward Nashville.

General Hood, in his book of campaigns that he has written styled "Advance and Retreat," says that "General Frank Cheatham was assigned to this duty, which he failed to do, and the enemy was permitted to pass on to Franklin without interruption." This has been denied in most positive terms by General Cheatham and his friends. Many strong articles have been written by soldiers whose opportunities to know were good, denying the fact as charged.

The next morning Hood resumed his march. Upon reaching Franklin, eighteen miles from Nashville, he found the enemy strongly intrenched behind a long line of breastworks. He immediately made his preparations to attack across an open field where one would conclude that a bird could not have survived the storm of shot and shell that swept across it. The divisions of Cleburne, Cheatham, Stewart, Bate, and Brown with their brave soldiers charged up to the enemy's breastworks, some of them reaching them and others going over them. They had done all that mortal strength and bravery could do, but had failed. Men were shot down on the field of Franklin, and while they lay in a helpless condition were shot again, some of them as many as three or four times. In a few moments General Hood had lost several thousand of his soldiers. More general officers were killed and wounded at Franklin than in any battle of our War between the States. Five of his generals were killed. Gen. Pat Cleburne was killed within a few feet of the works, with many of his division. Brigadier General Stahl, with his horse, was found dead on top of the enemy's works. Brigadier Generals Granbery, Carter, and Adams were also killed, and five or six other generals were wounded. A more daring exhibition of soldiers' courage was never made on any field-or by any army than that of the Army of Tennessee at Franklin on that chilly afternoon in November, 1864. General Hood was an eyewitness to all this, and I regretted and was surprised to read in his book the assertion that the Army of Tennessee had been so accustomed to fighting behind breastworks under General Johnston that they would not fight any other way. It is charitable to conclude that this was made while he was laboring under the sore disappointment occasioned by the failure to obey his orders at Spring Hill the night before, to attack the enemy if they attempted to move from Columbia. A Federal officer who commanded a brigade at Franklin, and now a member of Congress, General Sherwood, took occasion to say at the funeral obsequies of the late Gen. G. W. Gordon, Representative from the Tenth District of Tennessee: "Franklin was the fiercest, the bloodiest, and the most signal battle of the entire war."

The war histories tell us more of the two days' battle at Nashville, fifteen days later; but Nashville was a dress parade compared to Franklin. I was at the front in both battles. General Gordon was a brigadier general in command of a brigade at Franklin, and he was abreast of the front line of bayonets in that mad, wild, desperate charge. He was wounded and captured on the Federal breastworks. I quote the following from Colonel Vance's war history: "There was greater loss, greater sacrifice, and more bloody fighting on the part of old Frank Cheatham's men on that beautiful Wednesday afternoon, November 30, 1864, than took place on any field of the Crimean War. While thirty-seven per cent of Lord Cardigan's 673 men were killed or wounded in the memorable charge of the 600 at Balaklava, more than half of General Cleburne's and Brown's divisions were left dead or wounded in the fields and gardens of that little Tennessee town." In summing up, General Sherwood said: "More generals were killed and wounded in that six hours' struggle in front of Franklin than were killed and wounded in the two days' fight at Chickamauga or the three days' fight at Gettysburg, where three times as many soldiers were engaged. I have seen many battle fields, but never saw evidence of so terrible a conflict as at Franklin." I am glad that I have been able to use what General Sherwood has so truthfully, forcibly, and recently said in refutation of what General Hood has so unfortunately and unthoughtedly said in regard to the Army of Tennessee.

The Federals evacuated Franklin that night, falling back to Nashville, where General Thomas had collected a large army. General Hood followed in a few days, and by the 15th of December had placed his little army in front of Nashville, when a two days' battle ensued. It is sufficient to add here that after some hard fighting on the different parts of the long line presented by the Federals the Confederate lines were broken, and they were driven from the field in disorder.

The weather was exceedingly cold, creating much suffering among the soldiers. They were thinly clad, and many were barefooted, leaving bloody footprints upon the frozen ground. Many of them went to their homes to get clothing, some of whom never joined their columns again. Nothing like a vigorous pursuit was made, except between Pulaski and the Tennessee River. Quite a battle was had between the Confederates under Generals Walthall and Forrest and the advance guard of the enemy, in which the Federals were driven back with heavy loss.

General Hood crossed the Tennessee River near Corinth, Miss., with his broken and disorganized troops. In a short while he tendered his resignation, and Gen. Joseph E. Johnston was again called to the command of the Army of Tennessee. Thus General Johnston was reinstated by the same authority that had so summarily dismissed him a few months before. If anything could have relieved the gloom that was hanging over that army then, it was the reinstating of General Johnston.

Gen. John B. Hood was a brave and gallant officer. None made more reputation than he did while in command of a division in the Army of Northern Virginia. He had resigned from the United States army. He was elected colonel of the Fourth Texas Infantry, which was among the first troops that were hastened to Richmond on the breaking out of the war. He served through all the campaigns and battles of Virginia till he came with Longstreet to Chickamauga on the second and last day of that great battle, September 20, 1863. His division and that of General McLaws, numbering less than ten thousand, were all the troops of General Longstreet's Corps that arrived in time. He lost a leg at Chickamauga; and as soon as he had convalesced sufficiently he was given the rank of lieutenant general and assigned to the Army of Tennessee, which was then at Dalton, Ga., commanded by Gen. Joseph E. Johnston, just before the opening of the Atlanta campaign by General Sherman. I do not think that he was of the temperament to command an army or direct its campaigns. He was a tall, handsome man of commanding appearance, fully six feet in height, before he lost his leg. I have heard his couriers say that he would never dismount in battle, but would frequently call upon his staff and couriers to do so when balls were falling thick and fast about them. It was necessary for the commanding general to remain stationary close up to the battle line in order to receive and give the necessary orders as the fight progressed. At such times he would sit on his horse as calm and serene as though he were viewing a dress parade. Some years ago General Hood died in New Orleans of yellow fever. He had been in successful business there since the close of the war, and died one of its best and most respected citizens.

But to recur to the encampment of General Wheeler's command at Grahamville, S. C. We had not exhausted our Christmas supply of oysters before the enemy became very busy again, and we were ordered away to meet them. We had some fights at Pocotaligo and other places. They gradually forced us to the north and west. When we reached Columbia, they were hot on our track.

I have seen some controversy in late years about a fight that was had at a bridge on that side of the river. I do not remember about this; but I do remember passing over the bridge and going into the city, when the Fourth Tennessee was detailed as provost guard. We remained there all night, patrolling the place, with orders to leave at daylight, which we did. There was considerable excitement among the citizens; and at the depot, where we had a picket, a large amount of household goods were awaiting transportation. When we left, everything was quiet and orderly. Very few stragglers were found in the city, and we had them move on ahead of the command. The enemy came into the city as we moved out. We took the road leading north. When we had gone probably a mile from the corporation line, I looked back and saw dense smoke arising from the city. I remember that the sun was rising at this time. As we went on we could see the smoke thickening, and I supposed then, as I have concluded since, that Sherman's men did the burning, as it was in "accordance" with their purpose and acts after leaving Atlanta. It may be added that this has been a matter of controversy with some who have denied the fact. I only give my conclusions from what I consider the more reasonable evidence of the case. Why should the citizens of Columbia have burned their own property? If it was accidental, why did not a common feeling of humanity induce the Federal officers to order their soldiers to extinguish it?

General Wheeler continued to move northwardly toward Chester, Cheraw, and Winnsboro, S. C. We had some skirmishing and fights with the enemy's cavalry in which we held our own, giving as much as we received. A short time after this I remember that General Hampton assumed in person the command of our forces, and that he and Gen. M. T. Butler, both of whom were afterwards United States Senators from the State of South Carolina, riding at the head of the column in a forced march all night long, halted the column for a few minutes as the word was passed for all to stand still and make no noise. We had been there only a little while when we heard footsteps; and looking up the road, we saw some of our men passing us, having in charge a large picket of the enemy. We knew at once that something of a wakening character was at hand, and this was a signal for the men to arouse from their sleep on the ground and to mount their horses. We were soon in a rapid charge, and as daylight opened we found ourselves in Kilpatrick's camp.

The battle of Fayetteville, N. C., occurred on the 16th day of February, 1865, in the early morning. The battle field was some ten miles from the city. The soldiers who fought the battle speak and know of it as the Kilpatrick fight near Fayetteville, N. C. Many of the Federals had not arisen from their sleep; when we charged in among them, we concluded that we had the entire thing in our hands. Kilpatrick made his escape in his night clothes from a log house near the encampment; but we captured everything about his headquarters— a dozen horses, several carriages, and a number of attendants about the place. A few of his soldiers escaped on foot. Some of them commenced to fire upon us, and then there was a scattered fire for some little time. One column of our command was to make a charge and enter the encampment on our left. Unfortunately, they encountered a swamp, which occasioned a delay and some confusion, which caused the enemy to fire on us. Some infantry coming to the enemy's assistance, quite a battle took place, lasting for an hour or more, till, with further assistance from their infantry, they were able to drive us out of their encampment. We took with us five hundred horses and four hundred prisoners. The enemy lost a good many in killed and wounded. General Hume, in command of our division, Colonel Harrison, of our brigade, and Capt. Billy Sayers, his adjutant general, were so seriously wounded that they did not report for duty again during the remainder of the war. Lieut. Col. Paul Anderson, of the Fourth Tennessee, was also among the wounded. Lieutenant Massengale, of Company B, was killed with others, and quite a number of the Regiment were wounded. My opinion of this affair is: We did very well under the circumstances; but we would have done better had not the men commenced too soon a distribution of the captures, or had the other half of our command succeeded in crossing the swamp.

CHAPTER IX.

IN NORTH CAROLINA.

AFTER the wounding of the officers named in the foregoing chapter, Col. Henry Ashby, of the Second Tennessee Cavalry, succeeded to the position of major general of Hume's Division; Col. Baxter Smith, of the Fourth Tennessee Cavalry, to that of Col. Thomas Harrison's brigade; Adjt. George B. Guild, to that of Captain Sayers, as adjutant general of the brigade; Maj. Scott Bledsoe, to the command of the Fourth Tennessee; and Lieut. E. Crozier was made adjutant of the Regiment.

The enemy did not pursue us at once, and the command passed on to Fayetteville. We passed down the main street of the city and crossed the bridge that spans the Cape Fear River. As we passed over the bridge, I noticed that it had been rosined, and upon the other side near the bridge I noticed several cannons that had been masked. We were halted here. After a while we heard a considerable firing of small arms. In a few moments General Hampton came dashing over the bridge with a few cavalrymen trailing him. When he had crossed, the bridge was ignited, and soon the flames mounted the large frame structure, enveloping it in fire and smoke. A considerable number of the enemy's cavalry and infantry rushed down the street and into the opening on the other side, which was the signal for the battery to open upon them, which they did, rapidly throwing shells and shot into the dense mass, causing a scattering, falling down, and scrambling to get out of the way. It was too serious a matter to laugh at, but it really was amusing. Dr. Jim Sayers, of Company C of the Fourth Tennessee, was one of the squad that had come across with General Hampton. When asked what the firing meant preceding their coming over, he said that General Hampton had picked up about a dozen soldiers who were following the command, and, placing them in a turn of the street, awaited the coming of the advance guard of the enemy; and when the enemy had approached near enough, General Hampton and his men suddenly and unexpectedly dashed upon them with their revolvers, emptying some saddles, scattering and rushing them back upon the main line. He said that "General Hampton certainly killed several of the enemy in the mêlée, besides others that were killed or wounded."

Upon leaving here, we marched toward Bentonville, N. C. Gen. Joseph E. Johnston, who had been appointed commander in chief, had his headquarters near here and was arranging and collecting his small army to resist the advancing columns of the enemy, who seemed to be headed that way from every quarter. The railroads had been torn up in all directions,

Fourth Tennessee Cavalry Regiment. 127

and the Army of Tennessee was arriving in small detachments, traveling the distance from Corinth, Miss., partly on foot and partly by rail. Many of the absentees from Hood's campaign in Tennessee were joining in small squads. Some of them were captured in trying to cross the Tennessee, and some remained at home, giving up the contest as lost.

Soon after reaching Bentonville General Wheeler was ordered to Averyboro, N. C., to assist General Hardee. This took a day and night's march, if I remember rightly. General Hardee had taken position there to resist a column of the enemy marching toward Bentonville. Skirmishing was going on when we arrived upon the field. While awaiting orders Private Liter Herndon, of Company G, came up and asked permission to carry a battle flag that had been given us by a lady friend who happened to be at Winnsboro, S. C., as we passed through there a few weeks' before. It was a beautiful flag of fine material, said to have been made in Scotland. It was a Maltese cross, with eleven stars forming the cross of St. Andrew. We thanked the lady for the gift, promising her that it should be unfurled in our next battle. Remembering this, I asked Colonel Smith and his inspector general, Capt. J. R. Lester, to let Herndon have it, which was agreed to; and Herndon, cutting a sapling, attached the flag to it and soon disappeared. In a little while the brigade was ordered off to the right, where we were engaged in brisk skirmishing till nightfall, when we were ordered to our left front to relieve some infantry in a line of temporary works. We learned that the enemy were intervening between us and Bentonville, that General Johnston's little army was threatened, and that a battle was imminent. In passing up the road to the works, the rosin on the pine trees had been lighted, and we were visible to the enemy, who kept up a constant fire. As our infantry would pass us going to the rear, we heard more than one squad speaking of a soldier who had come upon the line that morning and said to them: "What are they keeping up such a racket for? I can see no one to fire at." Deliberately climbing over the works and, reaching an elevated position some distance to their front and mounting it, he waved his flag toward the enemy, who immediately turned loose a volley at him, and he and his flag fell to the ground. This brought to mind the incident of Herndon and the flag. When I inquired of the next soldier that passed, I was informed that he had been sent to the field hospital. I at once dispatched one of his company back to investigate the matter. I did not see him until the next day, when he reported the facts as stated, and that he found Herndon in the field hospital badly wounded in several places, and that one of the surgeons in charge told him that Herndon was mortally wounded and was certain to die. Before the friend left him, Herndon requested him to look in his haversack and get out the flag and return it to headquarters with his compliments. I have never heard of Herndon since, and I suppose that he died and was buried at or near Averyboro, N. C. This flag was afterwards most gallantly carried by James B. Nance, the bugler of the regiment, through the battle of Bentonville. The surrender of the army occurring a few weeks after this, Nance concealed the flag and brought it home with him to Smith County, Tenn. I have regretted since that I did not preserve the flag. I did not meet Nance for a year after we came home, when he said that he had given the flag to his wife and she had made an apron of it for her little girl. If I had it now, it could tell of more fire and battle, though short-lived as it was, than many of the flags we see so heroically flaunting at latter-day reunions.

A few days before the battle of Averyboro General Bragg, who was reporting to General Johnston, fought a battle at Kingston, N. C., with the Federal General Cox, driving him from the field with the loss of 1,500 prisoners and three pieces of artillery. At daylight we left the intrenchments at Averyboro, following General Hardee, who was hurrying on to Bentonville. When we reached Bentonville, the battle was on. General Johnston had had some success the day before, but the enemy were constantly arriving in great numbers.

This was the last general battle of the war fought

by the Army of Tennessee. General Johnston, in his narrative of his campaigns, says that his available forces at Bentonville were about 5,000 men of the Army of Tennessee, and that the troops of the department amounted to about 11,000. Sherman was marching against him with an army of 70,000, and nearly as large a force was approaching from the North Carolina coast. The last day of the battle, which, if I remember right, was the 19th or 20th of March, 1865, Wheeler's cavalry command was ordered to the front along a curved line that was to be extended from the right at a point on Mill Creek around to the left, so as to cover the small village of Bentonville and the bridge which spanned Mill Creek, a large and muddy creek with marshy approaches. The bridge was the only egress for the army. We moved along the curved line occupied by the infantry, and had hardly passed the crescent of the curve when we found General Johnston and his staff standing there in earnest conversation with General Wheeler. We heard Johnston order Wheeler to send a regiment to the left front and develop the enemy. The brigade commanded by Col. Baxter Smith happened to be in front, and Wheeler ordered him to send forward his front regiment, which was the Fourth Tennessee. Colonel Smith accompanied his old regiment, leaving the remainder of the brigade standing in line upon their horses in the edge of a wood. They had not proceeded far when, in passing over and down the slope of a hill, they came into the view of a line of the enemy's skirmishers extending for half a mile across the field. Upon seeing us, they commenced firing, and our horses and men were falling fast when the Regiment was ordered to dismount and the horses were sent to the rear. The men, moving out in the field to the left, threw down a fence and began firing upon the advancing skirmishers. We remained there some time, until it looked as if they would envelop us, when a courier came from General Wheeler with the order to fall back upon the line in the edge of the wood. As we moved back up the hill, the enemy continued to fire vigorously at us, and we could see our mounted men falling from their horses as we approached. The shots intended for us passed over our heads, killing and wounding many of them.

The courier who brought us the message to fall back was on horseback, and was shot in the head and instantly killed. His body was thrown into a passing ambulance, with directions to take it back to the village and bury it, marking the grave. He was Robert Davis, of Company K, and, though but nineteen years of age, had been in the war since its commencement. His father lived at Lebanon, Tenn., and soon after the war went to Bentonville and brought the body home. A gentleman had buried it in his garden, marking the grave. He had also kept his horse, and the father brought it home with him.

Johnston shifted his infantry farther to the left; the enemy coming no nearer, Wheeler was ordered still farther to the left. Here was encountered the enemy again in a sharp contest in a dense woodland. Among the wounded was Capt. J. W. Nichol, of Company G. This was the third wound that this most gallant officer had received. He was shot through the breast; and as he was borne from the field, pale and bleeding, it was remarked that we would never see him again. Remarkable to state, he was back at the surrender a few weeks thereafter, surrendering with his regiment. Colonel Smith had the Third Arkansas and the Eleventh Texas to dismount and march forward to where the skirmishing was going on. The Eighth Texas and the Fourth Tennessee were standing there in column. An officer of General Hardee's came riding in haste from down the road, and, inquiring for the officer, said to Colonel Smith that the enemy were threatening the bridge, and asked him to come down there as soon as possible, that such were the orders of General Hardee. Colonel Smith hastened with all dispatch with his two mounted regiments to the designated spot. The field hospital of General Johnston's army was close by; and as the command passed down the road, we could see men escaping from the hospital and a general scattering of men, evidencing that something of a stirring nature was happening. We found General Hardee standing in the road about half a mile or more from where we started. He at once ordered the regiments into line along the road and to charge through the woods, and, in coming up with the enemy, to drive them from the field. There was no force of our own in front of us, and there was a gap of a quarter of a mile or more from the creek to where our line extended from the right. We charged promptly and vigorously, as ordered, and had not gone far till we struck a long line of the enemy's skirmishers. They were taken by surprise at the suddenness of the attack; and as we rode in among them, using our "navies," we scattered them and forced them back to their main line, a distance of several hundred yards. Some were killed and wounded, and a few prisoners were taken. We lost a few men ourselves. At this juncture of affairs a line of our infantry appeared in our rear; and before the enemy could recover from their surprise we had a sufficient force to hold the position till General Johnston's army passed over the bridge that night. Undoubtedly this charge of the Eighth Texas and the Fourth Tennessee saved the bridge and made certain the escape of Johnston's little army at Bentonville, for at that time the enemy numbered six to our one. The enemy we were fighting was a large skirmish line of General Mower's division of infantry. General Hardee extended his thanks to Colonel Smith for the success of the gallant charge of his two regiments.

These facts I have stated were well known by soldiers of the army at the time, and I have frequently heard them expressed since. In late years some writers have written upon the subject, claiming that their respective commands took part in the fight on this part of the line. If they did, I am free to say that I did not see them, and my opportunities were good to know of it if they had done so. When the two regiments reached the point where General Hardee stood, there was some artillery firing toward the enemy from the right of our line and some artillery immediately in our rear that fired over our heads as we went down the slope into the wood. I remember that a piece of wood that had become detached from a canister shell struck Lieutenant Scoggins, of Company C, stunning him and making him unconscious for a while. He is now living in Nashville, and is one of its most prominent citizens.

This gap in General Johnston's line had suddenly become the most important part in the line, and all available forces were hurried there to repel the danger that seriously threatened: but I do not think any further firing took place. This was the last firing from the Army of Tennessee in its last battle during the war. General Johnston, in his report of the battle of Bentonville, says: "In the Eighth Texas Regiment, Lieutenant General Hardee's only son, a noble youth of sixteen, charging bravely in the foremost rank, fell mortally wounded. He had enlisted but a few days before." General Hardee reported his loss at Averyboro at 500. Prisoners taken said that the Federal loss was about 3,000. General Johnston, in his report on the three days' fighting at Bentonville, says that his loss was 223 killed, 1,467 wounded, and 653 missing. Of the missing, many of them reported to him afterwards at Smithfield, having charged through the Federal lines where gaps were made by the thick timber, and, passing into the country beyond, rejoined their commands in a few days thereafter. Maj. Buck Joyner, of the Eighteenth Tennessee Infantry, was one of this lot, who reported with about one hundred of his men. General Johnston, speaking further in his report on Bentonville, says: "We captured 903 prisoners." The Federals reported their loss to have exceeded 4,000, which is about correct, I suppose, when we remember that the Confederates fought for the most of the time in intrenchments. The appearance of the field of battle certainly justified such a conclusion.

My comment on the battle of Bentonville is that the Confederates fought with as much bravery and patriotic zeal as they had shown at Murfreesboro or at Chickamauga. It is true that they had everything to discourage them, had they stopped to think; but an instinct of honor suggested that they would stick it out to the end, let consequences be what they may, and the idea of a surrender had not then entered their heads.

CHAPTER X.

FURTHER MOVEMENTS IN NORTH CAROLINA, AND THE BEGINNING OF THE END.

AFTER the battle of Bentonville General Johnston retreated to Smithfield, N. C., a distance of seventeen miles. Gen. Frank Cheatham, with two thousand of the Army of Tennessee, joined him there, and small squads of that army continued from time to time to come up, marching on foot from Corinth, Miss. A lull took place in the movements of the Federal army at this time. Generals Sherman and Schofield had united their large armies, and were deliberating on their next movement to encompass General Johnston and his army. The Confederate recruits that had joined since the battle of Bentonville about supplied the losses Johnston had sustained during his North Carolina campaign.

During this lull in military movements General Johnston availed himself of the opportunity to reorganize his much depleted army. Five or six companies were consolidated into one, three or four regiments into one, and so on through the list to that of divisions. This, of course, retired many commissioned officers from the lowest rank to that of major generals of divisions. I do not remember that any lieutenant generals were interfered with, as I am of the opinion that we did not have an oversupply of this grade on hand. But to the honor of these retired officers, I did not hear of one who sulked in his tent for this reason; but they patriotically became members of the army again in some capacity, even down to enlisting, as many of them had done at the beginning of the war, as privates in their company. The infantry say to this day that most of them joined the cavalry. I know that some twenty of them, the highest rank among them being that of colonel, joined the Fourth Tennessee Cavalry and were paroled with that regiment. I remember after the reorganization to have met a soldier in the old Second Tennessee Infantry, and I asked him what was the number of his regiment since the reorganization. He replied that he did not know, as it was one of the questions that was past finding out; that he knew of a company of a lieutenant and five men that had been built up to the regulation limit of seventy-two men by the consolidation of five other companies and the enlistment of commissioned officers from the lowest rank to that of major general to reach the required limit. Of course the soldier was romancing, but really he was drawing a truthful picture of what the Confederate army was then, after four years of campaigning and fighting the battles that they had passed through.

Before General Johnston had left Smithfield he was officially notified of the fact that General Lee had been forced to leave Petersburg, Va., with his army on the 2d day of April, 1865. Richmond, the Confederate capital, had been evacuated, and the President and his Cabinet were then at some point in North Carolina, of which Johnston was notified by telegram, summoning him to meet them in conference. I do not suppose that any other officer of the Army of Tennessee knew of this fact at the time, even the highest ranking officers. While this conference was in session General Lee notified President Davis of the surrender of his army at Appomattox. I will be pardoned here for quoting liberally from Johnston's narrative for the purpose of showing what transpired at the interview between General Johnston and Mr. Davis and his Cabinet. The army was totally ignorant of all this, and the thought of a surrender had not entered their minds:

The three corps of the Confederate army reached Raleigh, N. C., on the evening of the 10th of April, 1865. In a telegram dated Greensboro, N. C., 4:30 P.M., the President directed me to leave the troops under Lieutenant General Hardee's command and report to him there. Taking the first train, about midnight, I reached Greensboro about eight o'clock on the 12th, and was General Beauregard's guest. His headquarters was a freight car near by and in sight of those of the President. The General and myself were summoned to the President's office in an hour or two, and found Messrs. Benjamin, Mallory, and Reagan with him. We had supposed that we were to be questioned concerning the military resources of our department in connection with the question of continuing or terminating the war. But the President's object seemed to be to give, not to obtain, information. He said that in two or three weeks

Fourth Tennessee Cavalry Regiment. 139

he would have a large army in the field by bringing into the ranks those that had abandoned them in less desperate circumstances, and by calling out the enrolled men whom the conscript bureau with its forces had been unable to bring into the army. It was remarked by the military officers that men who had left the army when our cause was not desperate, and those who under the same circumstances could not be forced into it, would scarcely in the present desperate condition of our affairs enter the service upon mere invitation. Neither opinions nor information was asked, and the conference ended.

General Breckenridge, as was expected, arrived that afternoon and confirmed the report of the surrender of the Army of Virginia. General Beauregard and myself, conversing together after the intelligence of the great disaster, reviewed the condition of our affairs, carefully compared the resources of the belligerents, and agreed in the opinion that the Southern Confederacy was overthrown. In conversation with General Breckenridge afterwards I repeated this and said that the only power of government left in the President's hands was that of terminating the war, and that this power should be exercised without more delay. I also expressed my readiness to suggest to the President the absolute necessity of such action, should an opportunity to do so be given me. General Breckenridge promised to make this opportunity. Mr. Mallory came to converse with me on the subject. He showed great anxiety that negotiations to end the war should be commenced, and urged that I was the person who should suggest the measure to the President.

General Breckenridge and myself were summoned to the President's office an hour or two after the meeting of his Cabinet the next morning. Being desired by the President to do so, we compared the military forces of the two parties to the war. Our force was an army of about 20,000 infantry and artillery and 5,000 mounted troops. That of the United States was three armies that could be combined against ours, which was insignificant when compared with either: Grant's army of 180,000 men, Sherman's army of at least 110,000, and Can-by's army of 60,000—odds of seventeen or eighteen to one, which in a few weeks could be more than doubled. I represented that under such circumstances it would be the greatest of human crimes for us to attempt to continue the war, for, having neither credit, money, nor arms but those in the hands of our soldiers, nor ammunition but that in their cartridge boxes, nor shops for repairing arms or making ammunition, the effect of our keeping the field would be, not to harm the enemy, but to complete the devastation of our country and the ruin of its people. I therefore urged that the President should exercise at once the only function of government still in his possession and open negotiations of peace.

The President then desired the members of his Cabinet to express their opinions on the important subject. General Breckenridge, Mr. Mallory, and Mr. Reagan thought that the war was decided against us, and that it was absolutely necessary to make peace. Mr. Benjamin expressed the contrary opinion, making a speech for war, much like that of Sempronius in "Soldier's Play." The President said that it was idle to suggest that he should attempt to negotiate when it was certain from the attempt previously made that his authority to treat would not be recognized, nor any terms that he might offer would be considered by the government of the United States. I reminded him that it had not been unusual in such cases for military commanders to initiate negotiations upon which treaties of peace were founded, and proposed that he should allow me to address General Sherman on the subject. After a few words in opposition to that idea, Mr. Davis reverted to the first suggestion, that he should offer terms to the government of the United States, which he had put aside, and sketched a letter appropriate to be sent by me to General Sherman, proposing a meeting to arrange the terms of an armistice to enable the civil authorities to agree upon terms of peace. The letter prepared in that way was sent by me to Lieutenant General Hampton, near Hillsboro, to be forwarded to General Sherman. It was delivered to the latter the next day, April 14, and was as follows:

Fourth Tennessee Cavalry Regiment. 141

"The result of the recent campaign in Virginia has changed the relative military condition of the belligerents. I am therefore induced to address you in this form the inquiry whether, in order to stop the further effusion of blood and devastation of property, you are willing to make a temporary suspension of active operations and to communicate to Lieutenant General Grant, commanding the Army of the United States, the request that he will take like action in regard to the other armies, the object being to permit the civil authorities to enter into the needful arrangements to terminate the existing war."

This note was promptly delivered to General Sherman, who agreed to the proposition and fixed the time for a conference. When they met for a secret interview, General Johnston asked that Gen. John C. Breckenridge be admitted to their meeting, which was also granted. On the 18th day of April, 1865, the two commanding officers of the respective armies agreed in writing as follows:

Memorandum or basis of an agreement made the 18th day of April, A.D. 1865, near Durham Station, in the State of North Carolina, by and between Gen. Joseph E. Johnston, commanding the Confederate army, and Maj. Gen. William T. Sherman, commanding the Army of the United States in North Carolina, both present.

This agreement contained seven different items relating to the terms of surrender, only one of which is necessary for our purpose to repeat here:

The Confederate armies now in existence to be disbanded and conducted to their several State Capitols, there to deposit their arms and public property in the State arsenal, and each officer and man to execute and file an agreement to cease from acts of war, and to abide the action of the State and Federal authority, the number of arms and ammunitions of war to be reported to the Chief of Ordnance at Washington City, subject to the further action of the Congress of the United States, and in the meantime to be used solely to maintain peace and order within the borders of the States respectively.

The seven articles of agreement close as follows:

Not being fully empowered by our respective principals to fulfill these terms, we individually and officially pledge ourselves to promptly obtain the necessary authority and to carry out the above program.

Both of the commanding generals attached their names to this paper, giving their official rank as commanders of their respective armies, and an armistice was declared, pending the transmission of the document to Washington City for the approval of the President of the United States.

CHAPTER XI.

THE END OF THE STRUGGLE.

WHILE the negotiations stated in the foregoing chapter were being had between Generals Johnston and Sherman Lieutenant General Hardee, who had been left at Smithfield in command of the Confederate army, commenced his move northward through Raleigh. The enemy, becoming active, moved also; but they did not come in sight until we were passing Durham Station, where we left the line of the railroad, marching in the direction of Chapel Hill. The enemy appeared in our rear and vigorously cannonaded the army as they passed, the cavalry bringing up the rear. First Lieut. H. L. Preston, of Company E, and First Lieut. Jo Massengale, of Company B, Fourth Tennessee, were left at Durham Station with their companies; and upon the enemy's advance guard coming up, they had quite a fight, in which both lieutenants, as well as some of their men, were wounded. This was the fourth time that the gallant officer Preston was wounded in action. Upon reaching Chapel Hill, Col. Baxter Smith's brigade was left there on outpost duty, the remainder of the army passing on. We remained at Chapel Hill two days or more, our headquarters being at a line of fence inclosing the college campus, and picketed the roads leading toward Raleigh, N. C.

The chaplains of the army were good men, and we could not have well done without their services. But I think they were generally "free lances" in the army, and were permitted to go and come *ad libitum* —at least ours was. One morning our chaplain came into the camp after a visit to the town of Chapel Hill, and told among the soldiers that General Lee had surrendered his army to General Grant at Appomattox. Of course a matter of such importance was quickly circulated through the camp. When Colonel Smith heard it, he sent a guard down and had the chaplain arrested and brought to his quarters. Upon being asked why he was telling so improbable a tale among the soldiers, he replied that he was only telling what he had heard fully discussed and told by the citizens he had met. The Colonel told him to consider himself under arrest and to take a seat.

Hardly fifteen minutes had elapsed before one of the pickets brought in a man, saying that he had been arrested while trying to get through the picket stand to go home, as he said that he had surrendered. Telling pretty much the tale that the chaplain had, he drew from his pocket a paper, which he handed to Colonel Smith, reciting the fact of his surrender under General Lee. It was a *bona fide* army parole, with all the earmarks upon it, leaving no doubt of the fact in the mind. He stated further that he had learned that an armistice was pending between the armies of General Johnston and Sherman looking to a surrender, and that we would be notified soon. The man under arrest was told to go his way; and then, turning to the chaplain, Colonel Smith remarked: "I reckon you, too, have gained your case without introducing a witness. You, too, can go your way." The same day we were notified of the pending armistice, and to come to a point beyond Ruffin's Bridge, at a crossroad, to go into camp awaiting further orders. It would be impossible to describe the surprise created from the highest ranking officer to the humblest private by this news. They were dazed, and had never thought of a surrender. It is surprising, too, that they had not; for they were too intelligent not to know of the disastrous condition of affairs, and that they were fighting a force numerically larger than their own by at least ten to one. Had they not concluded that all left to them was to remain to the end and to let consequences take care of themselves—in other words, that honor dictated that there was nothing for them to do but, if need be, to die with the harness on?

We at once marched to the designated encampment, going through Chapel Hill, crossing Ruffin's Bridge, and going into camp some twelve miles beyond it. We remained here, I suppose, ten days awaiting the return of the Johnston-Sherman capitulation. In the meantime the men took time to reflect, and had about settled down to the conclusion, after weighing all the facts, that this was about as favorable as they could expect, especially the second clause heretofore quoted—that they were to march home with their army accouterments, deposit them in their respective State Capitols, return to their homes, and obey the laws of the State and Federal authority. There was some show of recognition in this—that they were not to be considered as subjugated subjects, and were to return as veteran soldiers to their homes and families that many of them had not seen for four years.

During this interval the Third Arkansas and the Eighth and Eleventh Texas Regiments, whose homes were west of the Mississippi River, marched off home, saying that they were going to join Gen. Kirby Smith's army and fight it out over there. No discipline or restraint could be imposed at this time. They tried to persuade the Fourth Tennessee to go with them on account of the ties of true comradeship that had existed between them so long and during such trying scenes as they had shared together. A few did go; but better counsels prevailed, and the body of them remained, leaving Colonel Smith in command of a brigade of 250 men of the Fourth Tennessee Cavalry, besides about twenty of the relieved commissioned officers from the infantry who were reporting to him.

The time was spent in social visitation among the troops, the exchanging of addresses, and dreaming of home. We were invited to a dinner at General

Bate's headquarters, near by; but his negro servant, Ben, got drunk that day, and, unfortunately, we did not get as much dinner as we expected. The pine woods of North Carolina were flooded with old applejack, and the soldiers, of course, got their full supply of it. While we were at General Bate's headquarters an officer was seen at a distance in a field drilling his command as if the war had just started. Some one asked: "Who is that fool officer?" The reply came back that it was Gen. John C. Brown drilling his command.

This dream of home and loved ones was cut short one night when a mounted man inquired for Colonel Smith's headquarters. He was properly directed, and on coming up presented an order. Upon stirring up the fire to see, I read: "The armistice is over. You will take your brigade and go to or near Ruffin's Bridge and place your pickets covering the roads leading toward Raleigh." The company commanders were ordered to arouse the men, mount, and be ready to move out, as we had to go on picket duty. Of course many questions were asked as to what was up now. No answer could be made except that the order said that the armistice was at an end. In fact, before the Johnston-Sherman agreement could be acted upon, Mr. Lincoln had been assassinated by Booth. The Northern press, as well as the entire North, was asserting that the killing had been instigated by Southern citizens. There was a perfect storm of rage and frenzy, such, as has been said, that if an individual had expressed himself to the contrary he would have been torn to pieces by the wild and excited mob. Of course the treaty had been rejected, and hence the order to go on picket duty again. Silently and without saying a word, the 250 men of the Fourth Tennessee Regiment, all that was left of the brigade, moved out to the post of duty. They would have been taken for a funeral procession. These men had passed through hundreds of battles and skirmishes where blood had been drawn, and many of them had more than one battle scar upon their persons; but this was the grandest and noblest act of their soldier lives—still faithfully pursuing the line of duty when their star of hope had set forever. I remember that it was a bright moonlight night, and the shimmering light through the dense foliage of the forest of tall pines through which we were passing gave the scene a graveyard appearance. Nothing was lacking save the lonesome call of the whippoorwill or the mournful wailing of the night owl to have completed the picture. We reached the place to which we had been ordered. After the placing of the pickets, a courier came to headquarters with an order for Colonel Smith to repair to his former camp, as another armistice had been agreed upon.

On the 26th day of April, 1865, General Johnston surrendered his army of about 20,000 to General

Fourth Tennessee Cavalry Regiment. 149

Sherman. General Johnston had issued the following, which was read to the different commands:

Terms of a military convention entered into the 26th day of April, 1865, at Bennett's house, near Durham Station, N. C., between Gen. Joseph E. Johnston, commanding the Confederate army, and Maj. Gen. W. T. Sherman, commanding the United States army in North Carolina:

1. All acts of war on the part of the troops under General Johnston's command to cease from this date.

2. All arms and public property to be deposited at Greensboro and delivered to an ordnance officer of the United States.

3. Rolls of all officers and men to be made in duplicate, one copy to be retained by the commander of troops and the other to be given to an officer to be designated by General Sherman, each officer and man to give his individual obligation in writing not to take up arms against the government of the United States until properly released from this obligation.

4. The side arms of officers and their private horses and baggage to be retained by them.

5. This being done, all the officers and men will be permitted to return to their homes, not to be disturbed by the United States authorities so long as they observe these obligations and the laws in force where they may reside.

JOSEPH E. JOHNSTON,
Commanding Confederates.
W. T. SHERMAN,
Commanding United States Forces.

Supplemental terms of the same date, signed by these officers, recite among other things: "Section F. Private horses and other private property of both officers and men to be retained by them." General Johnston immediately after this issued his farewell address to his army, as follows:

General Orders, No. 22.

Comrades: In terminating our official relations I earnestly exhort you to observe faithfully the terms of pacification agreed upon and to discharge the obligations of good and peaceful citizens as well as you have performed the duties of thorough soldiers in the field. By such a course you will best secure the comfort of your family and kindred and restore tranquillity to our country. You will return to your homes with the admiration of our people won by the courage and noble devotion you have displayed in this long war. I shall always remember with pride the loyal support and generous confidence you have given me. I now part with you with deep regret and bid you farewell with a feeling of cordial friendship and with earnest wishes that you may hereafter have all the prosperity and happiness to be found in the world.

JOSEPH E. JOHNSTON, *General Official;*
KIMLOCK FALCONER, *A. A. G.*

The Confederate infantry received their parole at Greensboro, N. C., May 1, 1865. In order to expedite the printing and issuing of the paroles, the Confederate cavalry, under General Wheeler, was sent to Charlotte, N. C., where they received their paroles, dated May 3, 1865. General Wheeler issued the following farewell address to his cavalry corps:

Headquarters Cavalry Corps, April 28, 1865.

Gallant Comrades: You have fought your fight; your task is done. During a four years' fight for liberty you have exhibited courage, fortitude, and devotion; you are the victors of more than two hundred strongly contested fields; you have participated in more than a thousand conflicts of arms; you are heroes, victors, and patriots; the bones of your comrades mark the battle fields upon the soil of Kentucky, Tennessee, North Carolina, South Carolina, Georgia, Alabama, Mississippi, and Virginia; you have done all that human exertion

Fourth Tennessee Cavalry Regiment. 151

could accomplish. In bidding you adieu I desire to tender to you my thanks for your gallantry in battle and your devotion at all times to the holy cause you have done so much to maintain. I desire also to express my gratification for the kind feeling you have seen fit to extend toward myself, and to evoke upon you the blessings of your Heavenly Father, to whom we must always look for support in the hour of distress.

JOE WHEELER, *Major General.*

After this the troops scattered to their homes. The First Tennessee Cavalry Regiment, the Ninth Battalion of Tennessee, and a greater part of the Fourth Tennessee left in a body, as they resided in Middle Tennessee. We were provided with some rations; but after traveling some distance, we found that it would be necessary to forage upon the country. For the purpose of lightening the burden upon an almost impoverished people, we separated, the First Regiment and the Ninth Battalion taking the road to the right, crossing the East Tennessee Railroad at Strawberry Plains, and the Fourth Tennessee crossing at Sweetwater. At these places on the railroad the commands were halted, and an order was presented from General Stoneman (with headquarters at Knoxville) to dismount the men, take their horses, and ship the men by rail to their homes. Of course a protest was made against this proceeding, as it was expressly provided for by the terms of the articles of the surrender that the horses were the private property of the men and they were allowed to keep them. Forty years after this unwarranted proceeding the Congress of the United States passed an act to pay these soldiers for their horses and equipment—to wit: One hundred and twenty-five dollars for the horse and ten dollars for the saddle and bridle. This act was limited to soldiers that were paroled at the surrender of the Confederate army, and, in case of death, to their widows. Where there was no widow, the children were to receive the benefit. The act provided also that the taking must have been done by the United States soldiers. Many have availed themselves of this long-deferred justice, and in many cases it has benefited them and their families immensely.

About the 20th of May, 1865, the Middle Tennessee soldiers reached Nashville to proceed to their homes. It was a sad home-coming with many of them: to desolated homes, a war-swept country, families suffering for the necessities of life, and, worst of all, with a disreputable militia lording it over a helpless people, with the Freedman's Bureau playing an important part in the dirty work—in fact, it was their coöperator in chief. Many revolting acts could be told of its reign in Tennessee and throughout the South after the war.

CHAPTER XII.

Casualty Lists.

BEFORE closing this short narrative I have concluded to make a final effort to obtain a list of the casualties of the Regiment during the war. To get this now, forty-seven years after, I have been limited to very narrow resources; for but few men of the companies are living to-day, and they are old and feeble—many of them in mind as well as body. I have, however, seen a few personally and addressed letters to others asking information under the following heads: First, the names of such of their company as were killed in battle; second, the names of those that were wounded in battle; and, third, the names of those who had died of disease during the war. I thought I could and ought to present this much, if it could be obtained, that it might be preserved in form. I have succeeded partially in some instances. In one instance I cannot find or hear of a single soldier of the company who is living; in others very meager information is to be had. The companies composing the Regiment were from different and sometimes distant sections of the State. Those who have responded to the request have done fairly well in reporting the names of their company killed in battle, but the number of wounded and such as died of disease during the war it will be possible to give only in part. It is well known that every wound received in battle counts in making up a true casualty report. It is likely and probable that many of the wounded reported back in a short time, or maybe, as it was in many instances, that the men remained in camp till they had recuperated sufficiently for duty. In this way no general impression of their being wounded is made so long afterwards. But it is a universal and long-established rule in all armies that where one man is killed you can count with certainty that five have been wounded. Many of the men of the Regiment have been wounded more than once, some as many as four or five times, and in different engagements. In the conclusion I give I count only one wound.

I am selfish enough to say, and would not in any sense be extravagant, that the Fourth Tennessee Cavalry Regiment was one of the best in our army; that it had the fullest confidence of every general officer under whom it served, and was frequently called upon to do special and particularly important service. If the officers were alive, I feel that they would so testify if called upon. I would add that the Confederate cavalry were nothing more than mounted infantry; for in many of the hardest battles they were dismounted and fought as infantry, leaving their horses in the hands of the fourth man, which, of course, reduced their strength in battle one-

Fourth Tennessee Cavalry Regiment. 155

fourth. The dismounted men were left in charge of one or two commissioned officers, and were expected to stand at a safe and close-up position. To be a horse holder was not always safe, for to destroy or stampede the horse holders was a special object of the enemy. Shells were thrown among them when observed, and sometimes the enemy would quietly and secretly move to a position and attack them. I know that at times the dismounted men would have to go to the assistance of the horse holders. But the great damage was when their position was revealed and they were made a special target for artillerymen. Our cavalry was armed with the best of infantry rifles. Besides this, they carried in their belts navy or army pistols, which they used most dexterously and efficiently in mounted contests with the enemy. They ignored the regulation saber and threw them away when given to them, saying that they could whip any number of sabers with their six-shooters.

A partial list of the casualties in the Fourth Tennessee Cavalry Regiment is as follows:

FIELD OFFICERS.

Col. Baxter Smith, saber wound at Woodbury, Tenn., 1863; Lieut. Col. Paul F. Anderson, wounded at Fort Donelson, Tenn., 1863; Maj. Scott Bledsoe, wounded at Fort Donelson, Tenn., 1863; Capt. Marcellus Grissim, quartermaster, killed in Wheeler's raid, 1864.

COMPANY A.

Killed.—J. C. Bell, in Bragg's Kentucky campaign, 1862; James Reed, at Perryville, Ky.; W. J. Curren, at Morrison Station, Tenn.; Frank Crockett, at Morrison Station, Tenn.; W. J. Neil, at Morrison Station, Tenn.; Henry Allison, at Morrison Station, Tenn.; Sam Farrow, at Morrison Station, Tenn.; Z. Spencer, at Fort Donelson, Tenn., 1863; James Dark, at Chickamauga, Ga.; James M. Turner, at Newnan, Ga., 1864; Jessie Marlin, in Wheeler's Middle Tennessee raid, 1864; John Hopkins, at Perryville, Ky.; William Sandifer, at Resaca, Ga.; W. F. Lunn, at Perryville, Ky. 14.

Wounded (partial list).—Capt. D. W. Alexander, at Murfreesboro, Tenn.; First Lieut. A. R. McLean, at Tunnel Hill and Chickamauga, Ga.; Lon Fagan, at Fort Donelson, Tenn., 1863; Polk Hutton, at Murfreesboro, Tenn.; Jo Yarbrough, at Franklin, Tenn., 1862; Charlie Ransom, at Murfreesboro, Tenn.; Sam Waller, at Murfreesboro, Tenn.; W. R. Wynn, at Murfreesboro, Tenn.; George Slaughter, at Perryville, Ky.; John R. Mallard, at Buckhead Church, Ga., 1864; James Arnold, at Resaca, Ga., 1864; Billy Wilson, at Tunnel Hill, Ga.; Tom Fagan, at Fort Donelson, Tenn., 1863; Ben Nevels, at Fort Donelson, Tenn.; P. A. Lyons, at Griswoldville, Ga., 1864.

Died of Disease During War (partial list).—James Davis, James Gentry, David Watts, Tim Hare, Nick Oglesby, James Thompson, Newt Hargrove.

I hereby acknowledge the assistance I have had from Comrade Capt. R. O. McLean for a report of casualties of his old company. He made a visit to Marshall County to confer with the few surviving comrades before submitting the list. He was a citizen of Marshall County when his company was first organized, in 1861. He was then elected a lieutenant, when the company was sent to West Virginia, and he

Fourth Tennessee Cavalry Regiment. 157

served through the campaign Gen. R. E. Lee made in that section. The company returned to Tennessee in 1862. When the company was reorganized, he did not offer himself as a candidate; and when it was attached to and formed part of the Fourth Tennessee Cavalry Regiment, in 1862, he was made assistant to the quartermaster, Capt. Marcellus Grissim. When Grissim was killed, McLean supplied his place as quartermaster, surrendering as such at Greensboro, N. C., in 1865. He is now a well-known and active business man in Nashville, where he resides.

Company B.

Killed.—James Lindamond, at Murfreesboro, Tenn.; William Morrell, at Murfreesboro, Tenn.; A. A. Anderson, at Chickamauga, Ga.; William Wood, at Jonesboro, Ga.; James Cox, at Aiken, S. C.; Phillip O'Dell, at Waynesboro, S. C.; Second Lieut. Joe Massengale, at Fayetteville, N. C.; M. T. King, at Knoxville, Tenn.; — Hull, mortally wounded and died at Newnan, Ga. 9.

Wounded (partial list).—David Bushong, Henderson Avants, Nathan Avants, Jerry Luttrell, W. J. Godsey, Thomas Lester, J. Y. Snodgrass, C. C. Woods, A. L. Roder, J. T. Murrell, William Caline, H. H. Delaney (at Tracy City, Tenn., 1864), J. Sharp Ryburn, Third Lieut. Gideon Carmack, D. C. Carmack, J. A. Henlen, Abe McClelland (arm amputated at Bentonville, N. C.), William Sams, Henry Mattern, First Lieut. Joe Massengale (at Durham Station, N. C., 1865).

Dr. W. T. Delaney, the surgeon of the Regiment, assisted me in making out this list. He is now living at Bristol, Tenn., a man of wealth and high standing in his community. He was active and faithful in his duties, and is affectionately remembered by every member of the Regiment. Capt. C. H. Ingle, of Company B, was a brave and most excellent officer, and died in Virginia many years ago. He had been a member of the Virginia Legislature.

COMPANY C.

Killed.—William Trousdale, at Woodbury, Tenn.; Benjamin Burford, at Woodbury, Tenn.; Arch Modly, at Perryville, Ky.; Capt. Marcellus Grissim, in Wheeler's raid, 1864; Arch Roland, at Fayetteville, N. C.; Mack Paty, at Bentonville, N. C.; Joe Edwards, in Wheeler's raid, 1864; John Dillard, at Griswoldville, Ga.; James Green, at Morrison Station, Tenn.; John Bell, at Morrison Station, Tenn.; Tandy Sullivan, in Wheeler's raid, 1864; Esiah Gilliham, in Wheeler's raid, 1864; Dock Young, in Wheeler's raid, 1864; — Deadman, at Aiken, S. C.; George Curren, at Bentonville, N. C.; two men, names not remembered, killed at Perryville, Ky. 17.

Wounded (partial list).—Capt. George C. Moore; Lieut. James Hogan; Lieut. Robert Scruggs; J. A. Stewart, arm amputated at Newnan, Ga.; Joe Cato, arm amputated at Fayetteville, N. C.; Handly Gann, at Woodbury, Tenn.; H. L. Flippin, in Wheeler's raid, 1864; Elijah Tomlinson, at Woodbury, Tenn.

Died (partial list).—R. O. Donnell, George M. McGee, Jack Minton, J. N. Baker.

Lieut. R. L. Scruggs furnishes the foregoing list of casualties of the company. Lieutenant Scruggs is at present a well-to-do farmer in Smith County, Tenn. He is an intelligent gentleman and a devout member of the Church. He was wounded five times in battle, twice most seriously. We had no braver or more competent officer, and he was always at his

Fourth Tennessee Cavalry Regiment. 159

post when not absent on account of wounds. He is as good a citizen now as he was a true soldier when the war was on. He says that his company surrendered at Greensboro, N. C., numbering thirty-three, rank and file, and that all but three had been wounded in action, some of them more than once.

Capt. George C. Moore was well known in the Regiment as the "Old Reliable," and was always at his post. He died a few years ago at New Middleton, Tenn.

COMPANY D.

Killed.—Mart Robinson, at Fort Donelson, Tenn., 1862; Thomas Allen, at Duck River, Tenn. (Bragg's retreat), 1863; Clark Weaver, at Chickamauga, Ga.; Frank Mullinax, at Murfreesboro, Tenn.; John Gann, at Dake's Cross Roads, Tenn.; Mart Pemberton, at Fort Donelson, Tenn., 1863. 6.

Wounded (partial list).—Lieut. Bob Bone; Lieut. J. T. Barbee, three times seriously; Lieut. J. A. Arnold; Ord Richerson; Turner Johnson; Spencer Dillon; Newt Powell; Capt. J. M. Phillips, at Chickamauga, Ga.; Tom Floridy, at Chickamauga, Ga.; Tom Mont, at Chickamauga, Ga.; Hugh Jarman, at Chickamauga, Ga.; William Allen, at Readyville, Tenn.

Died (partial list).—Dick Odum, at Camp Morton (Ind.) Prison; Bill Knox, at Fort Delaware Prison.

Rev. J. T. Barbee, of Sturgis, Ky., has furnished the names of the few killed accredited to Company D. He has been for a number of years a minister of the Cumberland Presbyterian Church, and has held many high positions. There was no braver soldier in the army. He was faithful and true in every walk of life. He was wounded seriously two or three times in battle, and surrendered with his company at Greensboro, N. C., in 1865, with the rank of lieutenant. Lieut. J. A. Arnold has since furnished a few additional names. He is a resident of Wilson County, a well-known and most worthy citizen. He was in command of Company D at the surrender. First Lieutenant Barbee was acting commissary of the Regiment.

Capt. J. M. Phillips died at Nashville, Tenn., in 1910. He was a minister of one of the Baptist Churches of that city at the time. He was not with the Regiment after the raid into Tennessee, in October, 1863.

COMPANY E.

Killed.—John R. Rushing, at Aiken, S. C., 1864; Jack Nealy, at Aiken, S. C.; Legran Walkup, at Aiken, S. C.; Dan Porterfield, at Fort Donelson, Tenn., 1863; Tilman Tittle, at Fort Donelson, Tenn.; Joe Hare, at Aiken, S. C.; Tom Vance, at Perryville, Ky.; John Armstrong, in battle of Nashville, 1864; Tom Meely, in Middle Tennessee raid, 1864; Charles Milton, in Middle Tennessee raid, 1864; John Mitchell, in Middle Tennessee raid, 1863; E. J. Hawkins, in Middle Tennessee raid, 1863. 12.

Wounded.—Lieut. Hugh L. Preston, four times, last wound at Durham Station, N. C.; Tom Doak, at Atlanta, Ga.; Boney Preston, at Murfreesboro, Tenn.; A. W. Kennedy, at Fort Donelson, Tenn.; Nile Mitchell, at Chickamauga, Ga.; Lieut. John Fathera, at Chickamauga, Ga.

Died.—Burr Reid, in a Northern prison.

I am indebted to Lieut. Hugh L. Preston for the casualty report of Company E. He is now a worthy citizen of Woodbury, Tenn., and has represented his

Fourth Tennessee Cavalry Regiment. 161

constituency both in the Upper and Lower Houses of the Tennessee Legislature. He was young, active, and brave as a soldier, and was in every engagement of his company during the war. Perhaps he was absent for a short time, but only when suffering from wounds received in battle. He has the distinction to have been in command of those soldiers who fired the last guns before the surrender of the Army of Tennessee at Greensboro, N. C., April 26, 1865, which occurred but a few days afterwards. He is as worthy and honorable as a citizen as he was brave and true as a soldier.

Capt. H. A. Wyly, who commanded Company E, was as gallant in battle as he was intelligent and courteous as a gentleman. He died many years ago at his home, at Woodbury, Tenn. He was one of Woodbury's most worthy and public-spirited citizens.

COMPANY F.

Killed.—James Burke, at Chickamauga, Ga.; Jack Carder, at Saltville, Va.; John Dillard. 3.

Wounded (partial list).—Capt. James R. Lester, at Murfreesboro, Tenn.; Lieut. W. H. Phillips, at Tracy City, Tenn.; Lieutenant Burgess, at Murfreesboro, Tenn.; William Lester, leg amputated at Kennesaw Mountain, Ga.; Zack Thompson, at Lebanon, Tenn.; Kirk B. and P. Sherrill Harvey.

Capt. James R. Lester, of Company F, was a most gallant, dashing officer, handsome in person, and always rode the finest horse in the Regiment. He served from the beginning of the war, and was wounded several times in battle. He died some years ago at Lebanon, Tenn. He was a prominent and much-beloved physician. It is said that the wound received in the battle of Murfreesboro contributed materially to his death. When he surrendered at Greensboro, N. C., he was Acting Inspector General on the staff of Col. Baxter Smith, commander of the brigade.

COMPANY G.

Killed.—D. C. Witherspoon, at Perryville, Ky.; C. M. Webber, Triune, Tenn.; James Doughtry, in the Atlanta campaign, 1864; James A. Brandon, in Wheeler's raid, 1863; Joe A. Rushing, in South Carolina, 1864; D. W. Tolbert, in South Carolina, 1864; James Hughes, at Bradyville, Tenn. 7.

Wounded (partial list).—Capt. J. W. Nichol, three times, last at Bentonville, S. C.; J. E. Neely, J. C. Coleman, J. F. Dunn, W. P. Gather, John Gordon, John Harris, H. J. Ivie, Houston Miller, W. M. Spain, W. W. Grey, Lieut. John A. Sagely, Lieut. F. A. McKnight, Sergt. W. R. Fowler, A. W. Robinson, W. H. Youree, Walker Todd, A. R. Patrick, C. M. Roberts, L. M. Roberts, Sam Witherspoon, Isaiah Cooper, J. E. James, Lieut. Dave Youree.

Wounded and Died in Prison (partial list).—Lieut. J. A. Sagely, Calep Todd, Alfred Todd, Preston Carnahan, W. M. Bynum, D. C. Jones, Gid Martin, Arch Robinson, Jesse Robinson, John E. Jones, Frank Youree.

Capt. J. W. Nichol, of Company G, is the last surviving captain of the Regiment. Three were killed in battle, and the others have died since the surrender. He was dangerously wounded four times in battle, the last wound being received at Bentonville, N. C., the last general engagement of the Army of Tennessee, a few weeks before the sur-

Fourth Tennessee Cavalry Regiment. 163

render. It was thought at the time that his wound was mortal; but, to the surprise of every one, he was back with the company in a short time and surrendered with them. He had the distinction of having had a full company during the whole war. He was a thorough disciplinarian, obedient to every order, and was kind and attentive to the necessities of his men, who held him in high regard and respect. He is to-day an active business man at his home in Murfreesboro, engaged in commercial pursuits, an honorable and most worthy citizen. I am indebted to him for the casualty report of his company.

COMPANY H.

Killed.—Lieut. Allen B. Green, at Murfreesboro, Tenn.; Lieut. William Gaut, at Cedartown, Ga.; James Bennett, at Cedartown, Ga.; Moses Bennett, at Chickamauga, Ga.; James Carpenter, at Murfreesboro, Tenn.; Walter Magill, at Murfreesboro, Tenn.; James M. Pickett, at Cumberland Mountain, Tenn., 1863; Jack Smith, at Franklin, Tenn.; William Shell, at Mill Springs, Ky.; James Williams, at Perryville, Ky.; William Massengale, in Wheeler's raid, 1864; John Pickett, in Wheeler's raid, 1864. 12.

Wounded (partial list).—H. H. Harron, at Chickamauga, Ga.; Hickman Crouch, at Newnan, Ga.; Capt. Sam Glover, at Morrison Station, Tenn.; W. W. Warren, at Winchester, Tenn.; Thomas Godsey, at Morrison Station, Tenn.; Dan Jackson, at Chickamauga, Ga.; John McCall, at Morrison Station, Tenn.; James McDonough, arm amputated at Bentonville, N. C.; Richard Martin, saber wound, 1864; William Stone, at Fishing Creek, Ky.; Isaac Whitecotten, wounded four times in battle; O. K. Mitchell, at Murfreesboro, Tenn.; Robert Shumate, at Perryville, Ky.; Martin M. White, four times during the war.

164   *Fourth Tennessee Cavalry Regiment.*

Died (partial list).—William Cupp, at Chattanooga, Tenn., 1862; Pleasant Bell, at Knoxville, Tenn.; Levi Austin, at Knoxville, Tenn.; John A. Aiken, in prison, 1864; Jonathan Bailey, at Camp Chase, Ohio, 1864; Doc Cupp, at Chattanooga, Tenn., 1866; Charles M. Douglass, at Chattanooga, Tenn.; Arch D. Durham, in Georgia, 1864; William Goad, in prison, 1863; Rufus Godges, at Jasper, Tenn., 1862; John B. Hilton, in prison, 1864; Lieut. William Light, in Rock Island Prison, 1864; James M. Morris, in prison at Chickamauga, Ga., 1863; William Smith, in a hospital in Georgia, 1864; Houston Sutton, at Carthage, Tenn., 1862; Alex Tacket, in prison, 1864; David Thompson, 1862; Thomas Watkins, October, 1862; James B. Winder, at Gainesboro, Tenn., 1862; Alonzo Williams, in Kentucky campaign, 1862.

I am indebted to Comrade J. C. Ivey, of Company H, for the report from his company. He is living at Clear Lake, Tex., and is a prosperous farmer in that vicinity and a well-known and most respectable citizen. He is the only one who presents one of the last pay rolls of his company, which verifies fully the report he makes—facts that stand recorded at the time they occurred. He enlisted in his company at the beginning, and served continuously till the surrender, making an excellent soldier through his four years of service. I thank him for his response to my letter and his convincing report.

COMPANY I.

Killed.—Fentress Atkins, at McMinnville, Tenn., 1862; Cullom Jowett, at McMinnville, Tenn.; James Padgett, at Fort Donelson, Tenn., 1863; Elias Owens, at New Hope Church, Ga., 1864; Capt. Robert Bledsoe, at Sparta, Tenn., in Wheeler's raid, 1863; A. Bledsoe, at Sparta, Tenn., in

Fourth Tennessee Cavalry Regiment. 165

Wheeler's raid, 1863; Lieut. Foster Bowman, at Sparta, Tenn., in Wheeler's raid, 1863; Acting Adjt. E. Crozier, 1865; William Deason, Pleasant Poor, John Smith, Mike Hill, Lafayette Hill, and Robert Brown, in Wheeler's raid. 14.

Wounded (partial list).—Lieut. J. W. Storey, at McMinnville and New Hope Church, Ga., 1864; B. Porter Harrison, at Fayetteville, N. C., in 1865; James Singleton, at New Hope Church, arm amputated.

John W. Storey, now a prominent member of the bar at Harrison, Ark., furnishes the casualty list of Company I. He was the sergeant of his company for some time during the war, and was one of the best we had. As adjutant of the Regiment I never had trouble with his reports or the many orders made upon his company for information; they were always clear, concise, and exactly what was called for. He was made a lieutenant on the field of Bentonville for his bravery and efficiency in every duty as a soldier. He was in every engagement, and was wounded twice in battle, on both occasions seriously. I am also indebted to him for several valuable papers which he had preserved, and which he furnished to me.

COMPANY K.

Killed.—T. J. Allen, at Elk River, Tenn., 1863; Ed Hancock, at Munfordville, Ky.; Joe Barnes, at Murfreesboro, Tenn.; Jesse Horton, at Murfreesboro, Tenn.; John Bowman, at Murfreesboro, Tenn.; Robert Hearn, at Lebanon, Tenn.; James Hearn, at Tracy City, Tenn.; Joe Newsom, at Morrison Station, Tenn.; Jack McDonell, at Morrison Station, Tenn.; Ed Smith, at Kennesaw Mountain, Ga.; Andrew Van Trease, at Calhoun, Ga.; Joe Cammeron, at Grassy Cove, Tenn.; William Neal, at Marietta, Ga.; R. A. Davis, at Bentonville, N. C.; John Raine, at Manchester, Tenn.; Tobe Wharton, in Rock Island Prison. 16.

Wounded (partial list).—Lieut. William Corbett, at Chickamauga, Ga.; Lieut. DeWitt Anderson, at Rocky Face Mountain, Ga., 1864; Jack Barton; John Corbett, at Resaca, Ga.; George Farnsworth, at Tracy City, Tenn.; Jim Hearn, at Tracy City, Tenn.; William Stonewall, at Big Shanty, Ga., 1864; Frank Anderson, at Murfreesboro, Tenn.; Henry Nelson, at Crow Valley, Tenn.

Frank Anderson was under seventeen years of age when he enlisted in a cavalry company in 1861. He surrendered April 26, 1865, at Greensboro, N. C. So he saw and participated in all, from beginning to close. Company K was at first the escort of General Wharton, and afterwards of different commanding generals of the Army of Tennessee. Anderson was a great favorite, and was frequently called upon by officers to carry their orders to parts of the field where the battle raged hottest and fiercest. His character was that of a brave and reliable soldier. He has been an active and well-known merchant of Nashville, Tenn., since the war, and is still actively engaged in business. We are indebted to him for a full report of his company's killed in battle.

Company L.

Killed.—Capt. J. J. Parton, at Chickamauga, Ga.; Newt Cashius, at Chickamauga, Ga., 1863; — Bell, at Lookout Mountain, 1864. 3.

Wounded.—Lieut. William Henry.

Recapitulation: 112 killed multiplied by 5 equals

560 wounded, plus 112 killed equals 672 killed and wounded.

The Regiment never had a battle line of over seven hundred and fifty rifles, which diminished as the war progressed. Of the two hundred and fifty who surrendered at Greensboro, N. C., more than half of them had been wounded in battle, some of them more than once and in different engagements.

As stated before, I have taken extra pains to see and write to men of all the companies to obtain a list of the killed and wounded and those that died of disease during the war. I have been able to get a fair list of the killed in most of the companies; but I find it impossible, as they have said, to give the names of all the wounded and those that have died during the war. Imperfect as it is, I have thought best to publish such as have been given to me. I have delayed and kept open the list till the last minute, so anxious have I been to do justice to all. When we compare this list of wounded with the list of killed in battle, it is apparent upon its face that the greater number of the wounded have not been reported, so I am forced to apply the long and well-established rule in all armies of five wounded to one killed in battle, which is approximately correct. Aside from this, it will be seen from said reports that some comrades have been able to make but insignificant reports of their killed in battle. Every surviving member of the Regiment knows that they were as valiant in battle as their comrades of the other companies. It is their misfortune that none are left to testify for them.

The greater part of the companies in the Fourth Tennessee Cavalry Regiment had on their rolls as soldiers from 125 to 130 names. None of them at any one time had so many, but enlisted that many during the service. The nature of the service of a cavalryman carries him to different and distant parts of the country, giving him the opportunity to collect and bring to the company not only absentees, but recruits. The body of the Regiment was composed of active young men, born, as the saying is, upon horseback, which well fitted them for that arm of the service. More than that, they were lovers of the horse and rode only the best that could be had. In the Confederate cavalry the cavalryman had to furnish his own horse. It was not so in the Federal army. The government provided them with horses, and it could not be expected that he would give the attention to his horse that the Confederate would. This leaves us to say that the Confederate cavalryman did more effective and better service than the Federal cavalryman. There was no comparison to be made between the cavalry horses of the two armies. Generally speaking, the Confederate horse was of the best blood and make-up that could be found—in other words, he was purely bred from the best sires—while the Federal horse was pretty much of the rough order, large, inactive, and easily broken down and worn out. A good Confederate cavalryman would go hungry himself before he would permit his mount to suffer for necessary food. I have seen him time and again carry in a sack behind his saddle rations of corn hundreds of miles to meet an emergency rather than let his horse go hungry. I have seen him give a hundred dollars for six horseshoe nails and tack on the shoe himself rather than permit his horse to go lame. He and his horse consequently were always ready for active service, and it was this that made him more effective as a soldier than his enemy.

The greatest loss that the Regiment sustained was when the men were dismounted to fight as infantry; they were armed like the infantry and usually fought as infantry. I have said that upon the organization of the Regiment it numbered about one thousand, rank and file. It is also well to know that when a cavalry regiment is dismounted it loses one-fourth of its effective strength by its horse holders. The largest force the Regiment ever had in line on foot was about seven hundred and fifty. This was at Chickamauga, which occurred just after a two months' rest at Rome, Ga., when we took time to gather up all absentees and many recruits. Never after that did we have so many on foot as infantrymen.

It must also be taken into account that after the organization it was necessary to make many noncombatant details. Many were discharged for disability, from wounds received in action, sickness, etc. Others were discharged from being over and under the age limit. Many prisoners were taken by the enemy. The exchange of prisoners at all times was slow; but for two years or more before the war closed no exchange of prisoners was made, and I suppose that the Regiment had a hundred men who were not released from prison until after the war closed. And I am pretty sure that we had our share of those who got tired and "just quit fighting." All of these causes greatly reduced the line of battle; and of the two hundred and fifty that surrendered at Greensboro, N. C., April 26, 1865, at least three-fourths of them had been wounded in battle, and many of them more than twice in different engagements.

I have finished what I have to say forty-seven years afterwards. It is necessarily incomplete, for many things have faded from my memory, and I speak altogether from personal recollection. I have thought it proper to give a cursory history of the Army of Tennessee from the fact that the Fourth Tennessee Cavalry Regiment was a part of it, participating in all of its campaigns, marches, and battles from October, 1862, to the surrender, except Hood's campaign against Nashville. When General Hood left Atlanta, he ordered Wheeler to remain there and to march in whatever direction Sherman moved; hence we went to the sea, circumscribing as much as possible the burning and pillaging of Sherman's large army of seventy thousand. We met the Army of Tennessee again in North Carolina, and served with it till the surrender at Greensboro, N. C., April 26, 1865. I would have been pleased to mention the name of every gallant soldier of the Regiment, but it is now impossible to get it; and to name some and leave out others equally as meritorious would not be proper. I have had to speak of some who have given me valuable assistance in compiling the casualty list of their company. I trust that this may be a sufficient apology, and that no one will be in the slightest degree offended by the action.

CHAPTER XIII.

GEN. JOSEPH E. JOHNSTON AND OTHER OFFICERS.

THE Confederate army had five full generals, ranking in date of their commission as follows: Samuel Cooper, whose headquarters were at Richmond, Va., the capital, and who was never assigned to the field; Robert E. Lee, Albert Sidney Johnston, Joseph E. Johnston, and G. P. Beauregard. All of them had resigned from the United States army to join the Confederate States army.

Joseph E. Johnston was fourth on the list, but he was the highest ranking officer who had thus resigned. He was assigned to the command of the Army of Tennessee in 1864, when it had expended its greatest strength, there being no resources to draw upon. He was confronted by an army double the numerical strength of his own, with all the resources at hand that could be asked for. Much of the territory of the Confederate States and its most resourceful sections were in the hands of the enemy. The Mississippi River had been closed to Confederate navigation, foreign intervention had become a dead letter, the exchange of prisoners had indefinitely ceased, and the blockade of Southern ports completed the hope of receiving resources from the outside. Truly was the South hermetically sealed.

Who can say that the tactics assumed by General Johnston in his Atlanta campaign were not the best that could be used under all the circumstances? Or that, if he could have succeeded at all, it must have been by the military operations he adopted? Do not the operations of General Hood in a few weeks thereafter prove this to be true? For, after fighting a few battles around Atlanta, losing as many men as Johnston did in his campaign from Dalton to Atlanta, and then falling back to Jonesboro, thirty miles south, where he fought Sherman, all without material results, he then moved to the rear of Atlanta, continuing his campaign against Nashville, that terminated so disastrously. Again, were they not the same tactics that General Lee was inaugurating when he left Petersburg with his little army, retreating to Appomattox, which movement, we can see now, was made when it was too late?

I am not able to say what would have been the result of Johnston's proposed movement at Atlanta, but I can say this: that it promised more success than any that was attempted later. The restoration of General Johnston to the command of the Army of Tennessee looked as if Mr. Davis was repudiating his order of a few months before. General Johnston in accepting it displayed a magnanimity of character and patriotism never excelled. The army from which he had been so summarily dismissed was now shattered and broken to pieces, and the Confederacy itself was staggering to its downfall. His desire to share the fate of his soldiers and countrymen must have been the only motive.

When Joseph E. Johnston died, in 1891, a large and representative meeting of the citizens of Nashville was held in the First Presbyterian Church to do honor to his memory, and the following preamble and resolutions were unanimously adopted—to wit:

Mr. Chairman: Your committee to whom was referred the resolutions touching upon the life and character of Gen. Joseph E. Johnston beg leave to submit the following:

General Johnston died in the City of Washington on the evening of March 21, 1891. Society is so constructed that individual character becomes prominent and conspicuous by deed and action no less than by expressed thought. As we look back through the ages, we mark some names that shine as beacon lights along the way, whose characters we accept as prototypes of all their contemporaries. Joseph E. Johnston is the Confederate soldier's model—not from the fact alone that he was a good soldier, but time, having dealt gently with him, lengthening his days through the trying years that have passed since the war, has completed the picture, and as we behold the man we cannot but exclaim: "As grand in peace as he was valiant in war." It is hardly permissible by resolution to speak at length of our deceased comrade; and it is sufficient for this occasion to say that he was born in Old Virginia in 1807; was educated at West Point Military Academy, graduating thirteenth in the distinguished class of 1829, numbering forty-six graduates; was a lieutenant upon the staff of General Scott during the Indian War of 1832-36; was a soldier in the war with Mexico, was wounded three times in action, was promoted three times for gallantry during the war, and was carried from the field of Cerro Gordo desperately wounded; in 1855 was made Lieutenant Colonel of the First United States

Fourth Tennessee Cavalry Regiment. 175

Cavalry, and in 1860 was made a brigadier general and assigned to the position of Quartermaster General of the United States army.

Upon the secession of his State, he resigned the position and repaired to Richmond. He was the highest ranking officer who resigned from the United States army to join the Confederacy. He was placed in command at Harper's Ferry, at that time thought to be its most important position. He withdrew from the enemy's front at Harper's Ferry and came upon the field of Manassas in time to turn the tide of battle and rout the army of General McDowell. He was in command of the Army of Virginia in 1862 and resisted the advance of General McClelland as he approached Richmond by way of the Peninsula. He was seriously wounded at Seven Pines on the 31st of May, 1862, while leading his columns to the attack. This wound incapacitated him for service for many months. General Lee succeeded him in command of that army. General Johnston was in command in Mississippi for a short time, and in the first months of 1864 he superseded General Bragg in the command of the Army of Tennessee after the disaster at Missionary Ridge. It was here that he displayed his wonderful talent in reorganizing that army and bringing it to its highest state of perfection in a few months' time. When Sherman began his move on Atlanta in the spring of 1864, and as he approached Tunnel Hill, Ga., on his first day's march, the battle opened in earnest, and for seventy days and seventy nights its roar never ceased to reverberate. Outnumbered almost two to one, every flank movement of the enemy was met by a line of battle. At Resaca, New Hope Church, Kennesaw Mountain, and Marietta the heavy skirmishing resulted in battles, but in no instance in a general engagement. Some days upon the skirmish line and when the fighting would not rise to the dignity of battle the loss would be almost as great as the United States suffered in any battle in the war with Mexico. Well-authenticated battle reports show that General Sherman's loss on his march to Atlanta was fully 40,000, while Johnston's was less than 10,000. During the seventy days' fighting and moving from position to position it is a remarkable fact that no ammunitions or provisions of any description were lost, except some siege guns that were left at Resaca, having no transportation for their removal. The morale of the army was not impaired in any particular, and its movements were executed with the precision of a dress parade. No commander could have possessed to a greater degree the supreme confidence of his men, and no general rested more securely upon the courage of his soldiers.

Upon reaching the front at Atlanta in 1864, General Johnston was relieved and General Hood placed in command of the Army of Tennessee. It is impossible to express the surprise this order created, from the highest officer to the humblest private. A great calamity seemed to have spread itself over the army, and the developments a week or ten days thereafter confirmed the great mistake that had been made.

When the broken fragments of the Army of Tennessee assembled in North Carolina in the spring of 1865, General Johnston was called to its command again. A forlorn hope, indeed! His presence revived the spirits of those of his old soldiers who were left, and they felt strong and confident again, as was shown in the hotly contested battle of Bentonville near the close of the war. The end came in a few weeks thereafter. General Lee had surrendered at Appomattox. Two hundred thousand soldiers were concentrating under General Sherman, and nothing was left to Johnston but to surrender his less than 20,000 soldiers upon the best terms possible. In the negotiations that followed General Johnston showed himself to be a diplomatist and statesman.

In his farewell address to the army Johnston urged his soldiers "to observe faithfully the terms of pacification, and to discharge the obligations of good and peaceful citizens as well as you have performed the duties of thorough soldiers in the field." Such, in brief, is his military history. He was the last of the great commanders of the Army of Tennessee.

Albert Sidney Johnston fell at Shiloh, Gen. Braxton Bragg

died soon after the war, and Gen. J. B. Hood a few years later. Under their leadership the Army of Tennessee made its glorious history and won imperishable honor. The circumstances that molded the character of the soldiery who composed that army and the facts that precipitated the contest in which they fought can never exist again.

The people of this Southland give Joseph E. Johnston a place in their hearts and affections alongside those of Sidney Johnston, Lee, and Jackson. Memory's sweetest retrospect will be to contemplate the character of each, great and good, brave and honorable in their lives, and glorious in their death. Sleep on, great soldiers! Most of your lieutenants, with the long line of nameless heroes, have preceded you in crossing the river. Your names and fame will be secure in the keeping of grateful and admiring countrymen.

In summing up the public services of General Johnston, we conclude that as a civilian he had attained an honorable citizenship. He was called to represent Virginia in Congress, and was given high position in State and national affairs. He has discharged his trust ably, faithfully, and with an eye single to the public weal and the reëstablishment of the fraternity of the American people. That he was wounded seven times in battle attests his courage as a soldier. "Beware of Johnston's retreats" relieves him of its usual disaster. Aggressive at the beginning of the war, he was forced to accept the Fabian tactics, and we learned too late that if the Confederacy could have succeeded it must have been through this policy. His magnanimous patriotism cannot be overestimated when we see him again accepting, in North Carolina, the command of the broken and shattered fragments of his once well-appointed army. Therefore be it

Resolved by this vast assemblage of comrades and sympathising friends: 1. That we recognize in the life and character of General Johnston the noblest and highest type of the true Confederate soldier and American citizen, true to every profession and trust confided to his care. We commend his character as worthy of emulation, view his death as a national

178 Fourth Tennessee Cavalry Regiment.

calamity, and extend to the members of his bereaved family our condolence sincere and heartfelt.

2. That a copy of these resolutions be sent to his nearest kinsman.

       GEORGE B. GUILD, *Chairman;*
       W. H. JACKSON, J. H. HAYES,
       R. LIN CAVE,   J. A. RIDLEY,
       M. B. PILCHER, J. H. NEAL.

The Fourth Tennessee Cavalry Regiment served in Wheeler's corps after it was first organized in 1862 till the surrender. Maj. Gen. Joe Wheeler was a graduate of West Point Academy, and was assigned to the artillery, which is taken as an honor preferment at the Academy. He was among the first to resign from the United States army and tender his services to the Confederate government. He recruited an infantry regiment in Alabama and saw his first service at the battle of Shiloh. Immediately afterwards he was made chief of the cavalry, with rank of major general, and assigned to the Army of Tennessee. He was brave, energetic, and indefatigable in his efforts to obtain correct information of the enemy, their movements, their forces, and the topography of the surrounding country, for reliable information concerning these essentials was necessary. I have known him time and again to take a reliable squad and go in person on the most daring and hazardous excursions to obtain needed information.

Lieut. Gen. A. P. Stewart said to the writer since the war that General Wheeler was what a cavalry officer ought to be, the eyes and ears of the army;

that he excelled all cavalry officers we had in this regard; that he was obedient to orders, vigilant, prompt to act; and that the Army of Tennessee rested in perfect security when Wheeler was on the front. He fought many hard-contested battles during his four years of service, killing, wounding, and capturing thousands of the enemy. He conducted many of the longest and most successful raids against the enemy, notably the raid he made into Middle Tennessee after the battle of Chickamauga, when he burned one thousand of the enemy's wagons loaded with the richest stores, besides wounding and capturing more of the enemy than his own command numbered.

General Wheeler was a member of Congress from the State of Alabama when he was appointed brigadier general in the United States army and fought in the Spanish-American war. He fought the largest and most noted battle of the land forces on San Juan Hill, at Santiago, Cuba, in which he contributed more to its success than any other general, its result being the defeat and capitulation of the Spanish forces. Among the many notable cavalry generals I would enroll the name of General Wheeler next to that of Tennessee's great general, Bedford Forrest, and superior to him in many essentials as a great cavalryman. General Wheeler died in Washington soon after the Spanish-American War, where he had been serving the State of Alabama as a conspicuous Congressman for fifteen or twenty years, and was buried in the National Cemetery at Arlington.

Col. Baxter Smith, Lieut. Col. Paul F. Anderson, and Maj. W. Scott Bledsoe were respectively the field officers of the Fourth Tennessee Cavalry Regiment. Young, active, patriotic, brave in battle, each of them was called at times to the command and had the full confidence and support of the soldiers.

At the breaking out of the war Colonel Smith recruited a company at his old home, Gallatin, Sumner County, Tenn., and was elected captain of the company, which, upon organization, became a part of a battalion of cavalry of which James D. Bennett became lieutenant colonel and Baxter Smith major. Their first service was with Gen. Albert Sidney Johnston at Bowling Green, Ky. When Johnston evacuated the place, the battalion retreated with him to Shiloh and fought in that hotly contested battle. After the battle of Shiloh Major Smith was ordered to Knoxville; and when Gen. (then Col.) N. B. Forrest organized a command for an advance into Middle Tennessee, Major Smith was assigned to the command of a battalion of four or five companies that afterwards became a part of his regiment. They participated under General Forrest in that most brilliant battle at Murfreesboro, July 13, 1863, resulting in the capture of a large force of the enemy's infantry and artillery. A force much larger than that of General Forrest occupied Murfreesboro, and were all captured. On Forrest's return to McMinnville with his captures, he encountered a force of the enemy occupying a blockhouse at Morrison Station, on the railroad. Major Smith was ordered to dismount his companies or a part of them and take the blockhouse. They dismounted, and, charging up to the fort, twelve of them were killed and a large number of them wounded in a few minutes' time. They were repulsed, and that ended the affair. This affair taught the cavalry a lesson and afterwards they carried a section of light artillery with them on their raids. Major Smith's battalion accompanied General Bragg on his raid into Kentucky, participating in the battle of Perryville, and was at the capture and surrender of four thousand Federals at Munfordville. On Bragg's return to Tennessee, this battalion, with other companies, was organized into the Fourth Tennessee Cavalry, of which the gentlemen mentioned became the field officers. On reaching home immediately after the surrender, Colonel Smith moved to the city of Nashville to practice law, where he remained a well-known and successful lawyer, except for serving one term in the State Senate, till two or more years ago, when he was appointed one of the secretaries of the Chickamauga Park Commission, which necessitated his removal to Chattanooga, where he now resides. He is the only surviving field officer of the Regiment.

Lieut. Col. Paul F. Anderson was a native of Wilson County, Tenn., but a few years before the War between the States he was residing in the State of Texas. He attached himself to the Eighth Texas Cavalry Regiment, which was organized among the first Confederate troops, and went with that regiment to Gen. Albert S. Johnston's army, then at Bowling Green, Ky. He was with Colonel Terry, commanding the Eighth Texas, at Woodsonville, above Bowling Green, when that most gallant officer was killed. John A. Wharton, who succeeded Terry in command of the regiment, gave Anderson authority to go to his old home at Lebanon, Tenn., and recruit a company, which he did, enlisting the celebrated "Cedar Snags," composed of young men of the best families from the counties of Wilson, Davidson, and Sumner, afterwards becoming Company K of the Regiment. At the date of the organization of the Regiment Col. John A. Wharton had become a major general and took Company K as his escort. Anderson becoming lieutenant colonel of the Regiment, James H. Britton succeeded him as captain of Company K, both holding their ranks till the surrender, in 1865. Lieutenant Colonel Anderson was a brave and most gallant officer. To hear him talk one would conclude that he was too rash; but, really, he was one of the most discreet officers that were to be found. He knew better when to make or decline a fight than any officer of my acquaintance. His quaint sayings became proverbial in the army, and the infantry especially would cry out as he passed: "Here comes Paul." It seemed that he knew everybody and everybody knew him. I have heard Major General Hume, who was commanding the division, say to Lieutenant Colonel Anderson as he passed his line of battle: "Well, Colonel Paul, you know better than I can tell you what to do if the enemy approaches your line." Anderson was wounded slightly at Fort Donelson in February, 1863, and in the Kilpatrick fight at Fayetteville. A few days or a week before the surrender he was absent for some cause, and I do not think he was with the Regiment at the time of the surrender. I know that Colonel Smith was in command of the brigade and Major Bledsoe was in command of the Regiment. Anyhow, he had fought the fight to a finish and had won all the honors a parole could confer upon him. After the surrender he settled in Helena, Ark. He died there of yellow fever some years ago, greatly respected by the citizens, who buried him near the monument erected to Gen. Pat Cleburne.

Maj. Scott Bledsoe was a practicing lawyer in Fentress County, Tenn., when the war broke out. He was a descendant of the famed Bledsoe family that settled in Sumner County. He recruited and was elected captain of a company that afterwards became Company I in the Regiment. He, with his company, participated in the battle of Fishing Creek under the lamented Gen. Felix K. Zollicoffer, who fell upon that unfortunate field. The poet has most beautifully said of General Zollicoffer:

> "First in fight and first in the arms
>   Of the white-winged angel of glory,
> With the heart of the South at the feet of God,
>   And his wounds to tell the story."

Major Bledsoe, with his company, was in General Bragg's Kentucky campaign in 1862, returning with General Bragg to Tennessee. In October, 1862, when the Regiment was organized at Nolensville, Tenn., he was appointed major, and his company became Company I (as before stated) of the Fourth Tennessee Cavalry Regiment. He served continually with the Regiment until the surrender, and was in all of its battles and campaigns. His brother, Robert Bledsoe, afterwards killed in Wheeler's raid into Middle Tennessee, succeeded him as captain of the company. Major Bledsoe was a true and brave soldier and a most affable and intelligent gentleman. After the surrender he and many of his old company moved to other parts of the country. In fact, a local warfare existed in their section between the clans of Champ Ferguson on the Confederate side and those of "Tinker Dave" Beatty on the part of the Union men, and many revolting killings occurred. This lasted several years after peace was declared. Maj. Scott Bledsoe died at Cleburne, Tex., some years ago, one of its most prominent and wealthy citizens.

CHAPTER XIV.

AN ADDRESS AND A SPEECH.

THE Woodbury (Tenn.) *Press* of September 19, 1878, published the following upon the occasion of the first reunion of the Regiment after the war:

ADDRESS OF ADJUTANT GEORGE B. GUILD.

I rejoice in my heart to meet so many of you. More than thirteen years have passed away since, in the Old North State, by order of superior officers, you laid aside the equipments of war and furled forever the flag you have loved and followed—often in victory, sometimes in disaster, but always in honor and with a soldier's devotion to duty. It is meet and proper, fellow soldiers, that our reunion should be inaugurated at Woodbury. For here, under these towering hills and along the meanderings of the beautiful little river that laves your green and fertile valleys, were enacted many of the stirring scenes through which the Regiment passed. Here too it was our fortune to have encamped on outpost duty for some time. Who is it that does not remember with the fondest recollection the generous liberality of this hospitable people? Your male population were mostly in the army. The decrepit old men and women were here—God bless them!—and nobly did they extend a helping hand in every possible manner. This is the first opportunity we have had to return to you the thanks of our grateful hearts; and when I do so, I know that I utter the sentiment of every member of the Regiment. Amid all of the vicissitudes through which we afterwards passed, and the dreary years that have gone by since then we have remembered with gratitude, and with a longing for your prosperity and happiness, the good and noble women of this vicinity. In the name of the Regiment, I again extend our heartfelt thanks. It is meet and proper from another view that our inaugural meeting should be at Woodbury; for in this vicinity two of the Regiment's companies were recruited—Company E, Capt. H. A. Wyly, and Company G, Capt. J. W. Nichol. And while it would be improper to make distinctions when all have acted so well their part, two better companies never answered the bugle call or followed honor's beckoning. A hundred battle fields have been stained with your blood, and nowhere at any time has the slightest dishonor tarnished your fame as soldiers.

I see around me some of the surviving veterans of these two noble companies, battle-scarred, limbless, with the honors of war thick upon their persons; and it is well and proper that we should meet here amid friends and relatives of such men, to clasp again the friendly hand and open to each other the warm hearts of comrades while we talk of battles lost and won and renew that attachment for each other that germinated and ripened amid scenes that unmistakably told what stuff men are made of. Let this be an inauguration of a meeting together which shall extend through long years to come, having for its object the perpetuation of the truth of history, to preserve unsullied the reputation of the living, and to embalm forever the memory of those gallant spirits who offered their lives a free sacrifice to a cause which was as holy as that which nerved the arms of our Revolutionary sires. Let our children learn of it, so that they may teach their children's children that to have fought and lost does not necessarily stigmatize their ancestors as traitors. Might is not always right, and "truth crushed to earth will rise again."

But, fellow soldiers, it is no part of our coming together to discuss the theory of the War between the States—its causes or whether we were right or wrong. "There's a Divinity that shapes our ends, rough-hew them how we will." It is a stern fact that war did come and the most stupendous conflict of arms ensued of which modern history gives any account. Suffice it to say at this time that a strong sectional feeling had been engendered between the sections of the country; that it had originated many years before the war; and that it had grown in intensity year after year until 1861, when the war cloud became so heavily charged with angry passion that it burst in all its fury and enveloped the country in a conflict which, besides a million lives, cost an inestimable amount of property and treasure. Some of our sister States had been thoroughly instructed in the doctrine of State sovereignty. They had wrongs, grievous wrongs, to complain of at the hands of the North, which the North refused to remedy. They asked peaceably to retire from the Union of States. The government proposed to coerce them into submission and made her levies for armies upon sister Southern States for the purpose of whipping them into the Union. Not till this was done by the general government did Tennessee appear upon the scene. A few months before at the ballot box she had, by a majority of over sixty thousand, decided to cling to the Union of our fathers; but when she saw that it was to be a war of subjugation, she scorned to be neutral and elected to go with her people and kindred and to share their fate, be it for weal or for woe. Tennessee answered her sister States as Ruth did Naomi: "Whither thou goest, I will go; . . . thy people shall be my people, and thy God my God: where thou diest, will I die, and there will I be buried."

The drums beat, flags were unfurled to the breeze, sweethearts waved their handkerchiefs, and the boys went in. Ours was an unequal contest. It was a battle of the weak against the strong and powerful. The future historian, when he comes to tell the truth of history, will record it as follows: In point of numbers the Northern States were more than four times that of the Southern States. When we take into the estimate that some of these so-called Southern States contributed more largely to the Northern army than they did to ours, the disproportion in numbers can hardly be estimated. Not only this, but the North, before the contest was over, called to their assistance hundreds of thousands of foreigners and the negro slaves of the South. We withdrew from the Union, which left the government, with all its immense machinery, in their hands. They needed no recognition from foreign powers; we by our own strong arms had to win it. The accumulated national wealth of nearly a century was theirs—a powerful navy, the regular army, arms and ordnance of every description, with the machinery and workshops to manufacture more.

The South was an agricultural people. They had contented themselves with the production of the raw material, while they left it to the North to manufacture every article of use, from the smallest to the most important. They had to establish as best they could shops for the manufacture of every accouterment of the soldier and of every munition of war. There were not in the whole South a percussion cap manufactory or powder mill that could fill the cartridge boxes of a regiment of soldiers. There was no accumulation of supplies anywhere. There was not a single war vessel and but a few merchantmen in her harbors, and a drillmaster was as big a show as an elephant. I speak of this more particularly to refute the assertion that the South had for years been preparing for war. Not one word of it is true. Mr. Lincoln's proclamation was the electric spark that set fire to the house, and all the water in Christendom could not have quenched it. She did not stop to count the cost or to wait to get ready.

The Federal government proposed to subdue the rebellion in sixty days, and for this purpose sent forward toward Richmond the most magnificent army that had been seen on the continent, composed mainly of the regulars of the old army and officered by men of known ability and experience. It has been said that grand preparations had been made for a jollification over their anticipated victory, and that a large number of the citizens of Washington had accompanied the army "to see the fun." They were met at Manassas by a little over one-half their number of citizen-soldiers. A great battle was fought, which terminated in a most disastrous defeat and rout. Not until then did the Federal government comprehend the magnitude of their undertaking. New levies were made and the greatest expenditures entered upon. The South, too, marshaled her resources. It was a war between giants, and the full strength and capacity of both were brought to bear upon the result.

Great battles were fought from the Potomac to the Western borders, with varied results, for four years. I feel justified in saying that the South fairly won her proportion of these; but the difficulty with us was that we so expended our strength in battle that we were unable to follow up our advantage— that we had no reserve to call upon from the rear. This fact caused delay and enabled the enemy to draw upon their inexhaustible resources and repair the damage. In other words, we did not have the troops to follow up the success we had fairly won or to secure the prize within our grasp; while the enemy could in forty-eight hours (or in a very short time) hurry fresh men to their assistance, drawing not only from their own supplies, but from the mercenary population of foreign countries, with the slave population of the South thrown in for good measure. It could then be with the South but a question as to how long she could stand this letting out of her lifeblood. She stood alone and could look to no assistance from without. The principles of attrition were applied; and after more than four years of bloody war the South succumbed, but not to superior courage and soldierly bearing upon the field of battle. Her armies had been shattered and broken, and there were none to stand in their places. Numbers had told at last, and the fiery wave of battle had spent its force upon the beach.

We would not speak disparagingly of the soldier who fought against us, for to do so would be casting a shadow upon our own record. He fought well and bravely, and none other could have accomplished what he did. But the Northern soldier fought for conquest and subjugation; the Southern soldier fought for his home and his family. The one was an army of invasion, and the other was an army of defense. The Southern soldier fought more valiantly than the Northern soldier from the simple fact that he had more to fight for. But it is all over now, and it becomes us with charity to bury all the sad memories from our sight and to forget as well as we can all the heart burnings it engendered. "The past comes not back again. The present is ours; let us improve it and go forward to meet the shadowy future with manly hearts and without fear." This beautiful land is ours by birthright. Our fathers bequeathed it to us. We have an inalienable right to it, and in the language of Georgia's greatest orator: "We are here in our father's house. We are at home, thank God! We come charging on the Union no wrong to us. The Union never wronged the South. We charge all our wrongs to the higher law of fanaticism, which never kept a pledge or obeyed a law. We sought to leave the association of those who could not keep fidelity to the covenant. So far from having lost our fidelity to the Constitution, the South when she sought to go by herself hugged the Constitution to her bosom and carried it with her."

The privations you underwent while a soldier, the absolute sufferings at times for every necessity of life, the exposure to a summer's sun and heat and to the frost and snow of winter during your long and tiresome marches, nor have I mentioned the long, dark night of many of you in Northern prisons—the history of every civilized war pales into insignificance before it. The magnitude of your battles and the privations of your soldier life are without a parallel. Upon your battle flag is engraven "Murfreesboro, Chickamauga, Sequatchie Valley, Tunnel Hill, Dalton, Resaca, New Hope Church, Marietta, Atlanta, Newnan, Saltville, Griswoldville, Buck Head Church, Fayetteville, Bentonville," and to the list might be added a hundred other battles and skirmishes in which blood was spilled.

But the saddest memory of it all is when we remember the comrades who went with us but came not back. They saw "the blood-red sunset, and we are permitted to see the afterglow."

> "On Fame's eternal camping ground
> Their silent tents are spread."

They fell devoted but undying upon the battle fields of the far-off South, where their comrades placed them in their blankets in their shallow graves, which the rains of heaven or the plowshare have leveled with the earth. They are unknown but not forgotten. Their names are enrolled upon the hearts of a grateful and admiring people in letters of gold, and will not be forgotten.

I have been asked to insert in this book the dedicatory speech I had the honor of making upon the occasion of the unveiling of the Confederate monument at Mt. Olivet Cemetery in 1891. Rev. Dr. J. H. McNeilly, who was a true Confederate soldier, in a short time thereafter compiled and published a very neat pamphlet of the entire proceedings. Dr. McNeilly, though advanced in years and very feeble, still retains his love and admiration for his comrades, and is ever ready to lend his aid in the perpetuation of Confederate history. I will be pardoned when I say that I have been selfish enough to yield to this urgent request. The speech follows:

Comrades, Ladies, and Gentlemen: Tennesseeans are justly proud of their history. The daring exploits of their ancestry, who came across the mountains from Virginia and the Carolinas, read like a romance. Their early struggles with the savage and warlike foe and the important services they rendered the colonies in establishing American independence have stamped them as a race of men unexcelled in fortitude and courage. Subsequent facts justify the assertion that they imparted to their posterity all their high patriotic characteristics; for in the various Indian wars under Jackson, in the War of 1812 with Great Britain, in the Seminole War, and in the war with Mexico Tennessee played a most important part. We challenge the pages of history to show where the sons of sister States have done more—yea, as much—to maintain the honor, to broaden the public domain, and to establish the national power and greatness of the United States. Their valor won for them the proud name of "Volunteer State"; hence when our War between the States began, it was impossible for Tennessee to remain inactive. Being forced to a choice, they went with their kindred in blood and interest.

It is not within my province to speak at length of the soldiers—old and young, rich and poor—that crowded into the ranks of the Confederate armies. Tennessee furnished one hundred and eighteen regiments—about one hundred thousand soldiers, nearly one-sixth of the entire Confederate force. Many counties had more soldiers in the army than their voting population. For four years upon hundreds of battle fields they helped maintain the unequal contest. With resources exhausted and their armies depleted to skeletons, they lost all save honor. Three times during the four years' struggle were Tennesseeans driven from their homes and State; but they never thought once of deserting the flag or giving up the contest, though their homes were in possession of the enemy and their fields furnished them subsistence.

In 1862 they followed the fortunes of that great soldier Albert Sidney Johnston from Bowling Green to Shiloh, the field of his triumph and fall. They retreated from Perryville to Murfreesboro and Chickamauga under General Bragg. They fought under Gen. Joseph E. Johnston from Dalton to Atlanta, marking the route with the blood and graves of the enemy. At the command of Hood, they marched back to bloody Franklin and the vicinity of Nashville. From the Brentwood hills, with longing eyes and yearning hearts, they beheld the spires and domes of the beautiful capital of their beloved State. When overwhelmed with the torrent which Thomas turned upon them, with empty haversacks and naked, bleeding feet in midwinter, they followed their drooping standard beyond the Tennessee. When in the early spring of 1865 the broken and shattered fragments of the Army of

Fourth Tennessee Cavalry Regiment.   193

Tennessee gathered once more under the standard of Gen. Joseph E. Johnston in North Carolina, a large proportion of Tennesseeans answered to roll call, participated in the unequal battle at Bentonville, and surrendered at Greensboro.

Nor would we forget to mention in this connection the brave sons of Tennessee who fought in the Army of Virginia, who fought at Manassas under Stonewall Jackson, at Chancellorsville, at Gettysburg, and on other fields, and who, when overwhelmed in numbers, surrendered with Lee at Appomattox. The glory they so nobly won is a part of the immortal heritage of Tennesseeans.

A generation of men has come upon the stage of life since 1861, and the labor of many hands, multiplied by the passing years, has wiped away every trace of the awful conflict, but the story of the Confederate soldier still lives. It has formed an enduring lodgment in every home, and as the years recede its thrilling traditions will pass from lip to lip.

In May, 1865, the remnant of the Confederate army returned to their desolated homes. Since then there has been a desire on the part of this people not only to show to future generations their approval of the manner in which they performed their duty, but also to give some enduring testimonial of their appreciation of the honor and glory they won. This monument is the fulfillment of that cherished purpose; and now that it is finished, we trust that it will meet your approbation. At any rate, we ask you to accept it in the spirit that has created it. As its front inscription indicates, we dedicate it "to the valor, devotion, and sacrifice unto death of the Confederate soldiers of Tennessee." This generation need not be told what this means, for they too have lived under the dark shadows of the four years of blood and carnage. The tramp, tramp, tramp of the marching hosts echoes in their hearts to-day. Battle succeeds battle more deadly than before. Every messenger from the front tells of the wreck of a living hope. Every home is a house of mourning—a whole people baptized in martial glory, with one hope and one destiny.

This shaft is not intended to commemorate the fame of

our great generals—the account of the battle has told of them—but the private soldier, the rank and file of the Confederate armies, the citizen soldiery, who without hope of reward suffered privations, fought against greater numbers, and sacrificed their lives in the discharge of duty. From Gettysburg to the distant fields of the far South—wherever the army fought—they sleep in their blankets in unmarked and forgotten graves. It is their unwritten record we would lift aloft and inscribe their names among the stars. Driven from their homes, weary from forced marches, weak from hunger, in tattered garments, they marched to their death amid bursting shell and rattling, crashing musketry. Such we would remember to-day. And the lone sentinel yonder, as he looks away from the granite base, "instances each soldier's grave as a shrine." In the years to come let the stranger who is attracted to this spot, as he gazes up at that typical form, partake of the inspiration that we would have to linger here.

> "Pious marble! Let thy readers know
> What they and what their children owe
> To the brave men whose sacred dust
> We here commit unto thy trust.
> Protect their memory, preserve their story;
> Remain a lasting monument to their glory."

CHAPTER XV.

A Few Facts from History.

The Southern States furnished the Federal army with the following:

White troops	276,439
Negroes	178,975
Foreigners	444,586
Total	800,000

Foreigners in the Federal army were as follows:

Germans	176,800
Irish	144,200
British-Americans	53,500
English	45,500
Other foreigners	74,900
Total	494,900

The Federal army in its report for May, 1865, had present for duty 1,000,576, while it had present equipped 602,598. The Confederate army in its report for April 9, 1865, had 174,223 paroled and 98,802 in Federal prisons, making a total of 272,025.

As the armies stood at time of surrender:

Federal soldiers	1,000,576
Confederate soldiers	272,025
Total enlistment of Federal army	2,778,304
Total enlistment of Confederate army	600,000

1. The State of New York with 448,850 and Pennsylvania with 337,936 Union soldiers aggregated 768,635 soldiers and outnumbered the entire Confederate army.

2. Illinois with 259,092, Ohio with 313,180, and Indiana with 196,363 soldiers aggregated 768,635 soldiers and outnumbered the Confederate army.

3. New England with 363,162 and the 316,424 Union soldiers of the slave States aggregated 679,586 soldiers and outnumbered the Confederate army.

4. The States west of the Mississippi River, exclusive of Missouri and the other Southern States, enlisted 319,563, Delaware, New Jersey, and the District of Columbia 105,632, and the negro troops enlisted in the Southern States and not before counted were 99,337—an aggregate of 514,532 soldiers.

These facts, taken from the war records, show that there were four Union armies in the field, each of which was as large as the Confederate army.

The following list of killed and wounded (exclusive of prisoners) in the nineteen great battles of the war was compiled by Lieut. Col. G. F. R. Henderson, C.B., in his most excellent book of two volumes styled "Stonewall Jackson and the American Civil War." I am glad that some neutral party has so truthfully recorded the facts as they are. He came to the United States after the war in order to investigate and write for the benefit of an impartial public a true history. He was given every facility

Fourth Tennessee Cavalry Regiment. 197

for that purpose and had access to the reports of both sides, with the personal interviews of both Federal and Confederate officers who had participated from the beginning to the close of the war. After much labor and time spent, he made the following report, touching the killed and wounded of both armies in the battles named, which report received the full indorsement of Field Marshal the Right Honorable Viscount Wolseley, commander in chief of the Army of Great Britain. Taken, then, as such, it should be accepted as impartial and true.

LIST OF KILLED AND WOUNDED (NOT INCLUDING PRISONERS) IN
THE GREAT BATTLES OF THE WAR BETWEEN THE
STATES, 1861 TO 1865.

Name of Battle.	Date.	Number of Troops Engaged.		Killed and Wounded.			Total Percentage.	Percentage of Victor.
		Confederate.	Federal.	Confederate.	Federal.	Total.		
Manassas*	1861	18,000	18,000	1,969	1,584	3,553	9	10
Perryville	1862	16,000	27,000	3,200	3,700	6,900	16	
Shiloh	1862	40,000	58,000	9,000	12,000	21,000	20	20
Seven Pines	1862	39,000	51,000	6,134	5,031	11,165	12	9
Gaines Mill*	1862	54,000	36,000	8,000	5,000	13,000	14	14
Malvern Hill	1862	70,000	80,000	5,500	2,800	8,300	5	3
Cedar Run*	1862	21,000	12,000	1,314	2,380	3,694	11	6
Second Manassas*	1862	54,000	73,000	9,000	13,000	22,000	17	16
Sharpsburg*	1862	41,000	87,000	9,500	12,410	21,910	17	23
Fredericksburg*	1862	70,000	120,000	4,224	12,747	16,971	8	6
Chickamauga*	1863	71,000	57,000	18,000	17,100	35,100	27	25
Chancellorsville*	1863	62,000	130,000	10,000	14,000	24,000	12	17
Gettysburg	1863	70,000	98,000	18,000	17,000	37,000	24	20
Chattanooga	1863	32,000	60,000	3,000	5,500	8,500	8	9
S. River or M'boro*	1862–63	33,000	60,000	9,500	9,000	18,500	24	20
Wilderness*	1864	61,000	118,000	11,000	15,000	26,000	14	13
Spottsylvania C. H*	1864	50,000	100,000	8,000	17,000	25,000	16	16
Cold Harbor*	1864	58,000	110,000	1,700	10,000	11,700	6	8
Nashville	1864	39,000	55,000	3,500	3,000	6,500	6	5

*Indicates battles won by Confederates.

Confederates victorious, 12; Federals victorious, 7.

It will be seen from the report that the per cent of casualties (killed and wounded) at Chickamauga is greater than any other battle of the war—to wit: twenty-seven per cent. The next in order are Gettysburg and Murfreesboro, with twenty-four per cent each. It will be remembered, too, that at Gettysburg the combined armies engaged aggregated 163,000, while at Chickamauga the combined armies engaged numbered 128,000. The killed and wounded at Gettysburg numbered 37,000, while at Chickamauga the killed and wounded numbered 35,100—a difference of 35,000 in the aggregated strength of the two armies and only a difference of 1,900 in the number of killed and wounded. Gettysburg and Chickamauga were the two great battles of the war, as I have before remarked, the one in the East and the other in the West. In these engagements the Confederate army had its greatest strength and enthusiasm. After these two battles they fought with some degree of success to the last. The North continued to gather strength, while the South had no resources to draw upon. "The cradle and the grave" had made their liberal contributions, and for the soldier who fell in action there was no one to supply his place.

In the table I have indicated the Murfeesboro—or Stones River, as it is called by the Federals—battle as a victory for the Confederates when it should have been for the Federals. General Bragg gained a great victory at Murfreesboro on the 30th of December, 1862; but after two days' inactivity and failing to follow it up, he assaulted the fortified position of the Federals with a single division, that of General Breckenridge, who, after a gallant fight, was repulsed with heavy loss on the 1st of January, 1863. That night General Bragg withdrew his army and retreated to Shelbyville. Technically speaking, Colonel Henderson is correct, for the Federals had won every portion of the field at the termination of the battle.

I do not like to criticize any portion of what Colonel Henderson says in his report, but I am of the opinion that he is in error when he places the Confederate forces at Chickamauga as larger than those of the Federal army. I will do him the justice to say that I have heard the same claimed by Northern writers. The Confederate soldiers claim that the Federal army was numerically the largest. They account for the mistake in this way: It was well known that General Longstreet was ordered to Chickamauga to reënforce General Bragg with his large veteran corps from General Lee's army in Virginia, numbering some twenty or twenty-five thousand. But General Longstreet did not reach the field until the night of the 19th, and participated in the last day's fight, the 20th of September. Only two of his divisions reached there in time to take part in the last day's battle—the divisions of Generals

McLaws and Hood, numbering less than ten thousand. At a consultation had at General Bragg's headquarters on the night of the 19th the Confederate army was divided into two wings, General Polk to command the right wing and General Longstreet to command the left wing. More than two-thirds of the left wing were troops of the Army of Tennessee and were on the field before General Longstreet arrived. These facts show that the two armies were about equal numerically; if anything, the Federal army was the larger. The change of figures would adjust the relative strength of each army. Anyhow, there was honor and glory won at Chickamauga—enough to satisfy every American soldier that took part in that great battle. It was the deadliest battle not only of our War between the States, but stands without a parallel in all modern warfare. The great battle between Wellington and Napoleon at Waterloo, fought in 1815, falls short of it three per cent in killed and wounded, when the stake was the destiny of all Europe.

Since the war the government of the United States has purchased the entire battle field of Chickamauga (thousands of acres) and transformed what was a rugged and immense growth of timber and undergrowth into a beautiful national park, checking every point of interest with smooth roadways, and preserving at the same time every object as it appeared during the battle. A military post has been

Fourth Tennessee Cavalry Regiment. 201

established there, which the government is now about to enlarge at great expense. Troops from all the States, both North and South, participated in the battle of Chickamauga. Most of them have erected imposing monuments to their respective soldiers. A forest of monumental spires is to be seen in any direction one may travel over the great field of battle, every one of which, as it lifts its tall shaft to the skies, tells of the soldiers who fought there, whether they wore the blue or the gray.

As I have said before, the Confederate armies never enlisted more than six hundred thousand soldiers from first to last. I have said also that the Federal writers have denied this and claimed more, which under the circumstances they are more than anxious should be the fact. I still insist that the Confederate estimate—to wit, six hundred thousand —is approximately correct, as is shown in the June (1912) number of the *Confederate Veteran* in a well-digested and carefully prepared paper written by Rev. R. H. McKim, which most convincingly confirms these figures. President Tyler, of William and Henry College, writing on "The South in the Building of the Nation," says: "In round numbers the South had on her muster rolls from first to last about six hundred thousand soldiers." This estimate agrees with that of Adjutant General Cooper, whose duty it was to keep an accurate roster of the Confederate armies during the entire war; that of

Dr. Bledsoe, Vice President Alexander H. Stephens, Gen. Jubal A. Early, and Gen. John Preston; also with that of many other distinguished and reliable writers I could mention who confirm this estimate of the strength of the Confederate armies.

Every paroled soldier at Appomattox under General Lee on the 9th of April, 1865, or under Gen. Joseph E. Johnston at Greensboro, N. C., on the 26th of April, 1865, seventeen days afterwards, knew that he was fighting an enemy that outnumbered him from six or twelve to one. The Confederate paroled list, as well as the morning's reports of the Federal army, will show that this is an indisputable fact, and it should go down in history at these figures.

The latest United States census report made prior to the breaking out of the War between the States shows that the Northern States had a white population about five times as large as that of the Southern States. By the offering of large bounties, the United States enlisted four hundred and ninety-four thousand foreigners. Many of these at the close of the war never claimed citizenship here, but returned to the land of their nativity. Since the passage of the pension laws they have been paid millions of dollars by the United States. After nearly half a century the survivors are still drawing their pensions—mercenary soldiers in fact and in deed.

The Southern States furnished the Northern army

276,439 white troops and 178,975 colored troops. These are well-authenticated facts and fully justify Southern people for the insistence they make of the comparative strength of the two armies during the war.

We claim that no army has ever fought so valiantly as the Confederate army. All history fails to show a parallel case. For four years they maintained the unequal contest, fighting more and greater battles, conducting longer campaigns, and enduring more privations than were ever before recorded. The South claims this much, though in the contest they lost all save honor.

"No nation rose so white and fair,
Or fell so pure of crimes."

The Confederate cavalry regiments for three winters slept in the open air, without tents, before a log-heap fire. In case of rain or sleet, they would get some forked limbs, place a pole between the forks, put rails on the ground, resting them on the pole, and spread an oilcloth or blanket from the pole down to the ground. The result was a splendid "lay-out" (or "lay-in"), especially with the log-heap fire in front of the opening. The poet has exclaimed in ecstasy:

"Balmy sleep, tired nature's sweet restorer!"

One can never experience the sentiment unless this is tried. Some died in getting accustomed to it; but generally the survivors were stout, healthy, and active soldiers. A dry snow was not to be dreaded, for it supplied a covering equal to at least two blankets. When morning bugles were sounded, they would rise, throwing blankets and snow off them, feeling stout and strong enough to throw their horse over a ten-rail fence. Such a morning made the boys happy that they were Confederate soldiers and that they could dream of "home, sweet home."

Every survivor of the Confederate army will indorse what Gen. Bennett H. Young, Commander in Chief of the United Confederate Veterans, so well and truthfully said in his speech on Decoration Day, 1912, at Cave Hill Cemetery, Louisville, Ky., in part as follows:

Our love of country does not dim or tarnish the love for our Confederation. The Confederate States lived only four years, and they occupy upon the pages of human history more space than any other nation that lived for the same length of time. We are not ashamed for what they did; we rejoice in what we suffered. The glory and grandeur of the character of the Confederate soldier we shall maintain for all time. We have nothing to say derogatory to the courage, valor, and patriotism of our countrymen who sleep beneath the stars and stripes, and whose graves are kept green by a nation's gratitude and love; but we affirm that no nation of equal numbers, with the limitation of a large population of slaves, enlisted proportionately so vast a number of men under its standards or ever undertook to defend so vast a territory. We contend that no army of equal numbers ever fought so many battles in so brief a period or suffered such tremendous losses. One man in every three who wore the Confederate uniform died

Fourth Tennessee Cavalry Regiment. 205

on the battle field or from wounds received in conflict or in the hospital. History details no account of such a vast percentage of mortality or such tremendous sacrifices. These losses proclaim the incontestable valor of the Confederate soldiers, and no people who ever engaged in war inflicted upon their enemy such vast damage and injury.

But few remain of the line that went down with the flag on the 26th of April, 1865, at Greensboro, N. C. Another generation has come and gone since then. We seldom see each other now. May we meet again in the great hereafter!

> "In many a lonely thicket,
>   Far from life's beaten track,
> The scout and guard and picket,
>   The boys who never came back:
> They died where the cannon's thunder
>   Made savage pulses thrill,
> That the flag they battled under
>   Might wave o'er free men still."

CHAPTER XVI.

AFTER THE WAR.

THE assassination of President Lincoln was in a special way most calamitous to the citizens of the South. It intensified and augmented to the highest degree the angry passions engendered by four years of war and postponed for years that reconciliation of the two sections that the surrender of the Confederate armies should have brought about, happening as it did when the North was ablaze with bonfires in exultation over the downfall of the Confederate government; for General Lee had evacuated Petersburg, Richmond the capital had fallen, and its civil officers were fugitives.

The great crime committed by Booth was the act of a madman, born of the spirit that had suggested the burning of the ancient and famed Temple of Diana. Notwithstanding this, the Northern press teemed with the most exciting and inflammatory editorials, even charging well-known and most respectable citizens of the South and the officials of the Confederate government itself with complicity in the crime. Reason was dethroned, and it was unsafe to express a different conclusion.

At the South the act met with the most profound and pronounced condemnation, not only by the citizens of the South, but by the soldiers who had surrendered and were awaiting their paroles. I remember that when the information reached the army at Greensboro, N. C., one would have supposed that there would have been some indiscreet expressions or exultations, but instead of that it was received in silence and with pronounced expressions of the severest condemnation.

It is believed that if Mr. Lincoln had survived the war there would have been no such radical measures enacted and enforced as existed for years after the declaration of peace. The changed condition that the war had wrought was accepted in good faith by the people of the South, and the legislation necessary to adjust the autonomy of the seceded States would have taken place peaceably and at once. In fact, it is surprising that the good and just people of the North did not intervene to prevent this long period of misrule and the unlawful exercise of power and oppression. It is not my purpose to speak in detail of this now more than to say that I do not think a darker picture was ever spread before human minds than was presented during the long years of reconstruction in the South.

The first ray of sunshine to penetrate the darkness was when Brownlow's self-constituted legislature elected him to the United States Senate. It was well assumed that his counterpart could not be produced again. DeWitt Senter was Speaker of the

Senate and became Governor by virtue of his office. He was from East Tennessee and had been a consistent Union man, with no feelings of enmity toward his fellow citizens from whom he differed regarding public questions. Col. W. B. Stokes, a native of Middle Tennessee, was the logical successor to Brownlow. The Governor and legislature of the State were to be elected in a short time after Brownlow's election to the Senate, and Acting Governor Senter was a candidate for the office, as well as Colonel Stokes. To beat Stokes it was necessary to have another registration of votes, for as the poll stood Stokes was certain to be elected. Senter was fully aware of this; and having the power by law to ask for another registration, he did so, and at once issued indiscriminately to the voters of the State the necessary certificates. He was elected Governor, with a conservative, representative legislature. A constitutional convention was called, to which was elected by the whole people an able and representative body of men, who enacted a new State constitution in 1870 embracing the necessary amendments. In due time after this all obnoxious and oppressive laws were repealed by the legislature, and the State government was placed in the hands of its citizens again, which was the signal for the accumulated horde of vampires to fold their tents and march away in quest of a more congenial clime.

If there lingered in the minds of the people of

the North a feeling that the South was disloyal to the government, it was dispelled by the breaking out of the Spanish-American War in 1898, when they saw with what alacrity and unmistakable patriotism the Southern States answered the call made upon them for their quota of volunteer troops; and tendering at once more than were necessary, it could not but satisfy every doubting Thomas. Besides this, quite a number of the South's most noted generals during the War between the States tendered their services and were accepted by the President, valiantly assisting in bringing the war to a satisfactory conclusion. If that war effected no other result, it was sufficient, if not necessary, that it had happened in order to silence forever all doubt upon the question of the loyalty and patriotism of the Southern people.

The territory of the United States has broadened by the annexation of a number of new sovereign States. Its population in every section has been increased to a remarkable degree since the war. We feel that we are justified in saying that peace, prosperity, and happiness exist to-day throughout its borders. To extend these national blessings to future generations, we should remember that it can be done only by the enactment and enforcement of laws tempered with justice, founded in wisdom, and in sustaining the decisions of an incorruptible judiciary, which is the last and strongest hope of the liberty and freedom of the people.

The ex-Confederate soldier who faithfully performed his duty during the War between the States can now rest satisfied that the future historian will do him justice in his heroic effort to maintain the Constitution enacted by his rebellious forefathers and his attempt to enforce the decisions made by the highest tribunal of his country. He is as law-abiding to-day, nearly half a century afterwards, as he was then.

CHAPTER XVII.*

GENERAL BRAGG'S KENTUCKY CAMPAIGN IN 1862.

BY BAXTER SMITH.

IN June, 1862, after the retreat of the Confederate army from Corinth to Tupelo, Miss., in view of important movements to the northward had in mind by the Confederate authorities, it was deemed wise by General Bragg, who had succeeded to the chief command of the Army of Mississippi, to transfer Col. N. B. Forrest to Gen. E. Kirby Smith's Department of East Tennessee, in order that he might operate on Buell's line of communication with Nashville and Louisville, as well as Cincinnati.

At Tupelo the army was thoroughly reorganized by that master hand, Gen. Braxton Bragg, for an aggressive campaign into and through the State of Kentucky—one column under Gen. E. Kirby Smith, whose objective was Cincinnati, and one column

---

*I was not in the Kentucky campaign of Gen. Braxton Bragg in the summer and early fall of 1862. I have asked Colonel Smith to write it, as he was a major in command of five companies that afterwards formed a part of the Fourth Tennessee Cavalry Regiment, of which he was commissioned colonel at its organization, in October, 1862. In order that this narrative may present a full history of their services and his own during the war, he has contributed the interesting account in Chapter XVII.

under General Bragg himself, his objective being Louisville, Ky. While the Army of Mississippi lay at Tupelo, Miss., it was reorganized, drilled, and placed in a high degree of efficiency preparatory to its northward movement, which, when made, would necessarily draw General Buell from his base, then in North Alabama.

Pursuant to General Bragg's order, Colonel Forrest proceeded to Chattanooga, and from thence to the vicinity of McMinnville, where he organized his first brigade, consisting of about 1,300 men. Leaving Colonel Forrest at Chattanooga, I reported at Knoxville to Gen. E. Kirby Smith, who, when my credentials were presented, remarked that I was the man he was looking for. He at once commissioned me as major of cavalry and ordered me to repair to Loudon and take command of a battalion stationed there and join Colonel Forrest near McMinnville, which I did at once. After organizing the brigade and putting it in the best state of efficiency that could be done with raw troops, many of whom were badly mounted and armed and many of whom had never been under fire, the commanding officer called a council of war to determine what movement should be first made by the new brigade. Before this time efficient and trustworthy scouts had been dispatched to the vicinity of various important points along the Nashville and Chattanooga Railroad, it being deemed important to inflict as much

Fourth Tennessee Cavalry Regiment. 213

damage as possible to that road, which was the main line of communication of Buell in his expected retreat to Nashville and thence to Louisville. There were many important points along that road that were garrisoned, Murfreesboro, a city of from three to five thousand inhabitants, being regarded as the most formidable. A detailed account of the engagement there was made by me many years ago, and is as follows:

Colonel Forrest left Tupelo early in June, 1862, with a small staff, for the scenes of his new operations. Proceeding across the country to Knoxville, he reported to General Smith, who assigned him to the command of a brigade of cavalry, the various commands of which were ordered to report at a place known as Rock Martins, about seven miles east of McMinnville. There Forrest's first brigade was formed, and consisted of the Eighth Texas (Terry's Rangers) Regiment, commanded by Col. John A. Wharton; the Second Georgia Regiment, commanded by Col. J. K. Lawton; the First Georgia Battalion, commanded by Lieutenant Colonel Morrison; and a battalion consisting of four companies of Tennessee cavalry and a squadron of Kentuckians formerly of Helm's Regiment, all placed under the command of Maj. (afterwards Colonel) Baxter Smith. The entire effective force, armed, numbered about 1,300 men, all cavalry, many of whom had seen but little service, and what they would accomplish under their new leader had to be determined by testing them.

Reliable scouts were sent out along the railroad as far as and beyond Murfreesboro, and information of an important character was obtained, particularly of the situation at Murfreesboro. It was found that Murfreesboro was garrisoned by a force of about 2,000 men—two regiments of infantry, a battalion of cavalry, four new field pieces of artillery, and a company of 125 men.

With this information at hand, Forrest held perhaps his first council of war, where all the news brought in by scouts was laid before the council. All the field officers were present, as well as several citizens of distinction who were volunteer aides on Forrest's staff, among the number being Colonel Saunders; Hon. Andrew Ewing, a distinguished lawyer of Nashville; and F. C. Dunnington, former editor of the Nashville *Union*. As a result of the conference, at which it was evident that Forrest was the master spirit, it was determined to make a descent on Murfreesboro. The command was put in motion late on Saturday, July 12, with orders to "keep well closed up" and to make Murfreesboro by daylight the next morning, a distance of forty miles. After it had been determined to make a descent on Murfreesboro, Forrest had his brigade drawn up and made a stirring appeal to the officers and men to sustain him in the effort he was about to undertake. He told them that the next day (July 13) would be the anniversary of his birth and that he would like to celebrate it at Murfreesboro, near his birthplace, in a becoming manner. All of the commands promised that they would contribute what they could to the felicitation of the occasion. To Capt. Edwin Arnold, afterwards sheriff of Rutherford County, Colonel Forrest was indebted for much information connected with the expedition.

The command moved at a rapid rate, reaching Woodbury about midnight, where the whole population of the town seemed to be on the streets. The ladies of the town gathered about Colonel Forrest and related to him and his command the events of the evening before, when a large detachment of Federal soldiers had swooped down upon the town and had carried away almost every man, young and old, in the town, and had rushed them off to prison in Murfreesboro. These ladies appealed to Colonel Forrest in the most moving tones to rescue their husbands, fathers, and brothers and restore them to their homes, which he promised them he would do before sunset the next day, a promise that he literally fulfilled. Richard Cœur de Lion never made brighter resolve to rescue the holy sepulcher from the infidel when he donned his armor and went forth to battle with the Saracens than did Forrest on this occasion.

After partaking of a bountiful repast for men

and horses, the movement was rapidly resumed, Murfreesboro being still some eighteen or twenty miles distant. Reaching the vicinity of the city in the gray dawn of the morning, the scouts that had been sent forward reported that the pickets were stationed a short distance ahead. A small detachment was sent forward by Colonel Wharton, who was in the advance, and the pickets were captured, leaving an unobstructed road into the city. About this time other scouts reported that they had just returned from the city and had passed near all the encampments, that all was quiet and no notice of the impending danger seemed to have been given, and that they appeared not to apprehend it. Among the scouts performing this dangerous and important service were Capt. Fred James, a gallant soldier of Bragg's army and a native of Murfreesboro, who afterwards fell in sight of his home at the battle of Murfreesboro, December 31, 1862. Another was Capt. J. W. Nichol, who is happily spared to us. He afterwards, until the close of the war, commanded Company G (chiefly Rutherford and Cannon County men) in Col. Baxter Smith's Fourth Tennessee Cavalry Regiment. No truer or better soldier ever went forth to battle. He was wounded so often that it is doubtful if he knows himself how often, the last wound having been received at Bentonville, N. C.

Everything being ready, dispositions were made

for the attack, the expectation being to surprise the garrison. It was desired to attack the enemy at all points simultaneously. The first force to be encountered was the Ninth Michigan Infantry and a squadron of cavalry located on the Liberty Pike. The order was to form fours, the Eighth Texas to charge into the encampment in columns of platoons, which was executed in handsome style, and very shortly they were in the midst of the Federal encampment. The soldiers, for the most part, were in their tents enjoying their Sunday morning sleep; but they were very soon rallied and put up a sharp fight from behind wagons or any other protection they could find, many of them being undressed. In the first onset Colonel Wharton was wounded, as well as Colonel Duffield, the Federal commander. In the effort to rally his men, Colonel Wharton was at a disadvantage in that four of his rear companies, mistaking the orders, followed the lead of Colonel Morrison, who charged into the public square of the city, in the center of which stood the courthouse, which was garrisoned. After a sharp contest, the Eighth Texas withdrew on the McMinnville Road with a large number of prisoners, there being still a considerable portion of the Ninth Michigan in their encampment, which afterwards surrendered. Maj. Baxter Smith was ordered to charge the cavalry encampment, somewhat detached from the infantry, which was done. They were captured just as they were preparing to mount their horses.

While these movements were progressing, Colonel Morrison was ordered to take his battalion and charge upon the courthouse, which he did, taking by mistake four companies of the Eighth Texas, as already stated, and surrounding the courthouse, which was garrisoned by one company of the Ninth Michigan. This garrison was so well protected that they could not be reached by the Confederates from the outside, but the latter were picked off in every direction as they surrounded the courthouse. Among many others who fell here was the accomplished Colonel Saunders, of the staff, who was shot, the ball passing entirely through his body and one lung. After lingering long, he happily recovered.

There was much firing from houses and behind fences in different parts of the city where Federal soldiers were billeted or concealed and were practically in ambush. In this exigency Colonel Forrest came upon the scene, and the men hastily procured axes. The Texans and Georgians, led by Forrest, sprang forward in front of the courthouse, while Morrison brought up his men to the rear or west side. The doors were quickly battered down, and the Confederates swarmed inside and captured the garrison. It was found that the courthouse and jail were filled with citizens (about one hundred and fifty) of the town and surrounding country, including

Fourth Tennessee Cavalry Regiment. 219

those brought in from Woodbury the day before. These persons had been arrested and thrown into prison at the instance, mainly, of informers on various pretexts. Six of the number, some being men of prominence, were at the time under sentence of death, or, as expressed by a newspaper correspondent from there just before this time, were to "expiate their crimes on the gallows." Among this number was Judge Richardson, now an honored member of Congress from the Huntsville (Ala.) district.

By the time the courthouse was opened and there was a general delivery at the jail, whose doors were also forced open, the city seemed alive with people, including many of the families and friends of the captives, and the shouting and rejoicing that went up on that occasion will probably never be equaled in that community again. The cavalry and garrison at the courthouse had surrendered, but there was formidable work yet to be accomplished.

The Third Minnesota Regiment of infantry was stationed northwest of the city, near Stones River, and at a point near by were four guns that had been firing most of the day when opportunity offered. It was now past noon. Forrest made his disposition to attack the Federal forces in this quarter. Accordingly, he made a rapid detour to the right at the head of Major Smith's battalion and the Georgia troops and also a small company of twenty men under P. F. Anderson. Seeing the Confederates approaching, the Federals, then about five hundred yards south of their camp, halted and formed line of battle, there being some nine companies of infantry and four pieces of artillery. Directing the Georgians to confront and menace the enemy and engage with skirmishers, taking Major Smith with his battalion, which included the Kentuckians and three companies of Morrison's Georgians under Major Harper, Forrest pushed rapidly around to the right and rear of the encampment, which proved to be still occupied by about one hundred men posted behind a strong barricade of wagons and some large limestone ledges which afforded excellent protection. He therefore "ordered a charge, which was promptly and handsomely made, Majors Smith and Harper leading their men. They were met, however, with a stubborn, brave defense. Twice, indeed, the Confederates were repulsed. But Forrest, drawing his men up for a third effort, made a brief appeal to their manhood; and, putting himself at the head of the column, the charge was again ordered, this time with success. The encampment was penetrated, and the greater part of the Federals was either killed or captured."

The above in quotation marks is taken from Forrest's account of this part of the affair. An incident occurred at this point which has been grossly misrepresented, to Forrest's prejudice. While passing through the encampment he was fired at several times by a negro, who suddenly emerged from one of the tents. Forrest returned the fire and killed him, and did exactly what he ought to have done. This came under the personal observation of the writer.

The Georgians that had been left to confront the main body of the enemy, hearing the continued struggle in the encampment and mistaking it for an attack in the rear of the Federal force that they were confronting, charged in front, broke their line, and swept to the rear. Finding that the Federals quickly reformed their sundered line and held their ground firmly on an elevated ridge, from which position it was manifest that they would be hard to dislodge, Forrest thereupon promptly changed his plan of operation with that fertility of resource so characteristic of him. Placing Major Harper with his three companies so as to cut off retreat toward Nashville, disposing of Morrison's other four companies as skirmishers in front to prevent movement on Murfreesboro, and sending off the prisoners just taken on the McMinnville road, with munitions captured, Forrest led Lawton's regiment and Smith's battalion rapidly back to Murfreesboro, sending a staff officer at the same time for the Eighth Texas, which he found had gone about four miles out on the McMinnville Road.

It was now about one o'clock, and as yet little of

a decisive character had been accomplished, while among many of his officers there was manifest want of confidence in the final success in the movement. Some officers, indeed, urged Colonel Forrest to be contented with what had been accomplished. But, instead of heeding this advice, Forrest dismounted Major Smith's battalion and threw him forward with directions to engage in a skirmish with the Federal force that was still occupying the encampment of the Ninth Michigan. Lieutenant Colonel Hood, of the Second Georgia, at the same time was ordered to lead that regiment to a point to the left of the Federal position and prepare for a charge dismounted, while Colonel Lawton was detailed to write a demand for the enemy's immediate surrender.

All the while, as the report of Forrest shows, "Smith and his men were maintaining a brisk skirmish." Just as the Confederate demand was presented, Wharton's regiment came opportunely in view. The effect was most fortunate. Without further parley, and much to the surprise of many of the Confederate officers, the surrender was at once made of the Michigan regiment. This accomplished, detachments were made which collected the large wagon train filled with supplies most necessary, destroying what could not be carried off.

Colonel Forrest, with no loss of time, sent his adjutant, Major Strange, to the beleaguered Minnesota regiment, demanding its surrender. The colo-

Fourth Tennessee Cavalry Regiment. 223

nel of the regiment, Lester, asked to be allowed to interview Colonel Duffield, of the Ninth Michigan, who was wounded and was a prisoner at the Maney house, near where the Ninth Michigan was encamped. The interview was accorded; but Colonel Lester asked an hour's delay to confer with his officers, and was given thirty minutes, at the end of which time Forrest ostentatiously displayed his troops along the path that Colonel Lester was led in going and returning from his interview with Colonel Duffield, so as to make him believe that his strength was greater than it was. The object was accomplished, and just before night of that long summer day the last of the Federal forces at Murfreesboro capitulated.

This last surrender embraced the artillery. On account of the proximity of the large Federal forces at other points, Colonel Forrest had everything destroyed that could not be taken away, and by six o'clock his brigade was in motion for McMinnville.

The result of this affair was the capture of some 1,765 prisoners, including Brigadier General Crittenden, commanding the post, 600 head of horses and mules, forty or fifty wagons, five or six ambulances, four pieces of artillery, and 1,200 stands of arms. A Federal writer from Murfreesboro estimated their loss in property and munitions at one million dollars. In addition to the prisoners captured and taken, about one hundred stragglers came in the next day, and were paroled by Colonel Saunders, desperately wounded as he was.

After the troops and prisoners (together with the captured property) were put in motion on the McMinnville Road, Maj. Baxter Smith was ordered to proceed along the line of the railroad as far southward as Christiana and destroy the bridges, then to return to Murfreesboro and destroy the bridges across Stones River. This order was executed, resulting in the destruction of the bridges and the capture of a small garrison guarding a bridge some five miles from the city. The last of these orders was executed about midnight Sunday night, and Murfreesboro was unoccupied by soldiers of either army, except the wounded, who could not be carried away.

After Forrest's brilliant engagement at Murfreesboro (which made him a brigadier general), he made proper disposition of his prisoners. After a rest of a day or two, the command, including my battalion, to which, previous to the battle, were attached two splendid companies of Kentuckians commanded by Captains Taylor and Waltham, was put in motion toward Lebanon, some fifty miles distant, at which point it was reported that a Federal force of some five hundred men were stationed. Marching day and night, Lebanon was reached about dawn July 20, to find that the enemy had heard of our approach in time to escape. No more hospitable treatment could have been accorded the soldiers than was given by the splendid citizenship of this old, historic town. The noble women of the town vied with each other in superb entertainment.

On the next day the command was moved in the direction of Nashville, thirty miles distant, then strongly fortified and garrisoned by a large Federal force under command of General Negley, as well as the redoubtable Military Governor, Andrew Johnson. To lend inspiration to the troops, a party of irrepressible young women with escorts appeared on the scene near the Hermitage, twelve miles from Nashville, to celebrate the anniversary of the battle of Bull Run, being well supplied with edibles for their picnic, to which the soldiers were invited, and many spent an enjoyable hour.

At a point on Stones River about seven miles from Nashville a picket force was captured, as well as a small picket force near the lunatic asylum, driving the balance into the city. Simultaneously with these operations a small Confederate force, probably under Duvall McNairy, without any concert of action with Forrest's command, dashed on the Federal pickets and drove them in on the Franklin Road, producing the belief in the city that it was surrounded and threatened with a serious assault. The long roll was called, and general preparations were made in the city to resist the assault.

Pushing forward to Mill Creek, four miles from the city, which was spanned by a bridge, we assaulted the small force which guarded the bridge, capturing some twenty prisoners and destroying the bridge. Antioch, about one mile distant, was next attacked. We captured some thirty-five prisoners, destroyed the depot, stores, and freight cars, and burned the bridges. Part of the command was here detached and moved in the direction of Murfreesboro, destroying a bridge, capturing fifteen more prisoners, and killing and wounding about as many, without sustaining any loss.

After Forrest's capture of Murfreesboro, General Nelson was sent out from Nashville with an infantry force of about 3,500 men, which vainly tried to come up with Forrest, marching and countermarching, finally landing at Murfreesboro, giving up the chase in disgust. General Forrest then moved to McMinnville and halted for rest and observation of the enemy's movements till August 10, when the main army under General Bragg moved, from which point the command, being threatened with a superior force, fell back to Sparta. Meantime General Bragg had established his headquarters at Chattanooga, where he was concentrating the Army of Mississippi for his contemplated campaign into Kentucky.

General Forrest next moved from Sparta to Woodbury, to the enemy's rear, threatening Murfreesboro. From there the command moved up the railroad, destroying all the bridges and tearing up the railroad track near McMinnville.

Near Altamont the Federals had almost surrounded Forrest's small force; but by superior strategy he escaped, leading his brigade back to Sparta, which place the advance of General Bragg's army had already reached. This was early in September, 1862. After being reënforced by four companies of cavalry of his old regiment and a section of artillery, Forrest was assigned the duty of guarding General Bragg's left flank and rear, he being now in full movement for Kentucky.

My command moved along the line of the Louisville and Nashville Railroad practically all the way from near Nashville to within about six miles of Louisville, destroying bridges and tearing up the track. After reaching Louisville, Forrest was ordered to report to General Polk. Under Polk's orders we moved to Munfordville in time to prevent the escape of a large force of infantry (3,000 or 4,000 men) and artillery in the fort at that point. This movement of General Forrest compelled them to return to their fortifications, which soon afterwards were assailed by the Confederate infantry and artillery and compelled to surrender. I rode into the fort with the officers who received the capitulation. The whole of Bragg's army came up in the meantime, and it was the general opinion that he ought to give battle to General Buell at that place, it being in his direct line of march to Louisville, and for many other reasons. But he thought differently and turned aside toward Bardstown. About the 25th of September General Forrest was ordered to turn his brigade over to Col. John A. Wharton, his senior colonel, of the Eighth Texas, and proceed at once to Murfreesboro to take command of the troops that might be raised in Middle Tennessee.

A summary of the operations and casualties of the brigade up to that time showed that its killed and wounded amounted to 200 men. We had killed and wounded of the enemy fully 350 and captured over 2,000 prisoners of war, including one brigadier general, four or five field officers, about sixty regimental officers, four pieces of artillery, two stands of colors, six hundred draft animals, and a large wagon train.

As the army of invasion under General Bragg entered Kentucky in the month of September, 1862, it soon became understood that Col. (afterwards General) Joseph Wheeler had the confidence of the general commanding in a very eminent degree, and that he would have the chief direction of the movements of the cavalry arm of General Bragg's army in Kentucky, the arm of service with which I was connected. This was particularly so after General (then Colonel) Forrest returned from Bardstown, Ky., to Murfreesboro, Tenn., he having taken leave of his brigade at Bardstown, turning it over to Col. John A. Wharton, who was afterwards justly promoted to the offices of brigadier and major general.

Fourth Tennessee Cavalry Regiment.   229

No army ever marched forward with higher hopes of success and more eager for the fray than did the Army of Mississippi move into Kentucky. The forward movement from the swamps of Mississippi, to which General Beauregard had retreated from Corinth, seemed to inspire the troops with new life and to have imparted vigor and health to many a wasting form. Many a pale-faced and emaciated boy who had been reared in the lap of wealth in the blue-grass regions of Kentucky and Tennessee took heart when he turned his face homeward, and resolved that he would not die with the diseases that were so prevalent in the army at Tupelo at that time. It is too familiar to all to render it necessary to mention that the movement into Kentucky was accomplished by flanking General Buell, making a detour by way of Chattanooga and Knoxville, the right wing of the army, under Gen. E. K. Smith, moving by way of the latter place, and the remainder of the army, under the immediate command of General Bragg, by way of Sparta, Tenn., with a view of striking General Buell's communications a short distance north of Nashville and of pushing as far as possible on that line toward Louisville. General Smith moved first. He made a most brilliant fight at Richmond, Ky., completely routing the Federals under General Nelson and capturing 5,000 prisoners. He moved on to Lexington and pushed on to Covington, opposite Cincinnati. The first that I saw of

Colonel Wheeler on that campaign was near Franklin, Ky., when he was throwing every obstacle to be conceived in the way of the enemy's march to check or hinder his progress. Every bridge on the road, however small or insignificant, was destroyed, and the railroad track was torn up all along the way.

The main army of General Bragg moved up the Louisville and Nashville Railroad as far as Elizabethtown, and there turned off to Bardstown, to the right. Here the infantry and artillery rested and recruited some two weeks, while the cavalry, under Colonels Wheeler and Wharton, pushed on as far as possible on all roads toward Louisville. I went within six miles of the city, and was there when, in view of an expected attack on the city, so great a panic prevailed as to cause a majority of the women and children to be sent across the Ohio River. When the main army left Bardstown, it moved in the direction of Perryville, and there it formed a junction with a portion of the forces of General Smith.

While the army rested at Bardstown the cavalry pushed as far forward as possible toward the enemy on all roads from that point, and skirmishes with the Federal cavalry were almost daily occurrences. General Bragg beat no hasty retreat from Bardstown, but left leisurely to join General Smith, and intended then to give battle or retire from Kentucky into Tennessee with the rich spoils accumulated in this "land of milk and honey." As the Federal army advanced the cavalry gradually fell back until we were within a few miles of Bardstown. As a matter of strategy and as an illustration that some of our adversaries relied upon tricks and unfair advantages in their military operations, I will add that, while skirmishing with the enemy on the Louisville Pike, a flag of truce party appeared in my front, and I immediately ordered all firing to cease. As I understood it, the rule was that when either side sent a flag of truce and it was received it operated as an injunction upon all further movements of the army, pending the flag of truce. I received the officer with courtesy, and he presented an official communication addressed to General Bragg, sent for no other purpose, in my judgment, than to ascertain the movements of the army and General Bragg's whereabouts. I forwarded the document to Colonel Wharton, commanding my brigade, who forwarded it to General Bragg. The captain in command of the flag of truce party said that he would wait for an answer, and did wait probably two hours.

During the time, however, I discovered, what I at first suspected, that his object and that of the Federal commanding general was not only to learn the whereabouts of General Bragg, but likewise to advance their whole army under cover of this flag. I had some men posted at some haystacks on the left, and there were some houses near by. The first we discovered of their treachery was that their skirmishers suddenly dashed forward to these houses, and I immediately opened fire upon them to prevent their reaching the houses. At the same time I placed the captain and his cavalry escort under arrest and informed the officer that I considered the truce violated, and that they were my prisoners until further orders. They readily yielded and affected great mortification that there should have been a change in the position of their army pending the flag of truce.

After some explanations from a General Smith, who commanded the Federal brigade in my immediate front, and who came down in person, the flag of truce party was released, and each side agreed to retire a certain distance. My orders were to retire to a certain point which would be the outpost for the present, and I was not to skirmish any in retiring. Notwithstanding this agreement, I was to witness the crowning act of perfidy on the part of the enemy, whose cavalry made a sudden dash in superior force on my left and captured Lieutenant Scruggs and ten men. I felt the loss of this brave officer and his trusty men keenly. It was now night and very dark, and nothing further could be done.

On the next morning Colonel Wharton wrote a very strong note in reference to this perfidious act, addressed to Major General Thomas, commanding the division in our front. Maj. Tom Harrison and I were sent with an escort under a flag of truce to a stone house, probably five miles from Bardstown, and there delivered the communication. We were detained there at least two hours, at the expiration of which time we received the reply of General Thomas that he would consider the case when he got into camp, and this was the last of the captured party for some months.

We kept our obligation on this day, as on the day before. The Federals violated theirs, as on the day before, and, pending this flag of truce, moved their whole army forward; and while we were waiting for a reply a cavalry brigade, by making a wide detour, threw themselves between Colonel Wharton's brigade and Bardstown, and their infantry support was only a short distance behind. We had orders from Colonel Wheeler to encamp in Bardstown that night, and were taking it leisurely in marching there when a Texas Ranger who had been on a "bread detail" stumbled upon the Federals between us and Bardstown and gave the alarm. We were completely "cut off" from the remainder of the army.

No time was to be lost, and but one course seemed to be left open to pursue, and that was to make a determined dash at them and sweep every obstacle from our way. Colonel Wharton did not hesitate to take this course; and, putting himself at the head of his brigade, he ordered: "Form fours, and charge!" Soon we were sweeping down the pike like an avalanche, and presently we came in sight of the bluecoats forming in a long line covering every approach to the town. The impetuosity of that charge, however, stimulated by that wild yell peculiar to the Southerner, was not to be resisted; and after delivering one or two volleys, which did not check our boys, their whole line gave way, and they fled from the field in utter confusion, and their officers were never able to get them to stand again, although the infantry was almost in supporting distance. Nothing could have been more handsomely done, and it was accomplished with slight loss. The number the enemy lost in killed, wounded, and prisoners was considerable. I cannot state the number. Each of our boys seemed to have felt it to be a duty to bring away a prisoner or a horse, and I saw many a hatless cavalryman riding behind the Southern boys on horses that they had lately claimed as their own.

Capt. Mark Evans, of the Eighth Texas Regiment, was as brave a spirit as I ever knew. I shall never forget his exploit of unhorsing two of the enemy in almost an instant and the pleasure that he seemed to derive from recounting the circumstance to me that night. Poor fellow! he was destined to fall in the next conflict we had, which was only a few days later, at Perryville.

Fourth Tennessee Cavalry Regiment. 235

From Bardstown we moved on toward Perryville, checking the enemy's advance as much as possible. At Perryville it was apparent to General Bragg that the enemy must be checked in order to give him time to move off his baggage train and stores, as well as those of General Smith. I will not attempt a description of that bloody encounter, lasting from about 2 P.M. until 8 P.M. General Bragg had only about 12,000 or 14,000 men engaged, while the enemy had two large corps, Gilbert's and McCook's. The country is beautifully undulating, and chain after chain of hills meet the eye, reminding one of the waves of the ocean. As the Southern forces advanced the Federal troops receded. The enemy was forced back at least two miles. It was deemed by General Bragg that the enemy's advance had been sufficiently checked, and he commenced his famous retreat from Kentucky.

It was in this retreat that Colonel Wheeler, who had chief command of the cavalry, particularly distinguished himself. So untiring and sleepless was Wheeler's vigilance that General Bragg moved leisurely out of the State with his trains intact and without the infantry being called upon. The battle of Perryville was fought on the 8th of October, 1862; and the pursuit was kept up as far as London, in Eastern Kentucky, which our rear reached about the last day of October. It was on this retreat that I became well acquainted with Colonel

Wheeler and found him to be a thorough soldier. As gentle as a woman and as chivalrous as a cavalier of the olden time, he possessed the finest courage, and could generally be found with the rear guard as the enemy advanced, personally seeing that nothing was omitted necessary to check the enemy's advance. His habits were strictly temperate, and he usually lay down to sleep at night with his men in bivouac.

At London Colonel Wheeler ordered me to take the troops that I was then in command of as major and proceed on the road which passed through the Cumberland Mountains at Big Creek Gap, to cover the right flank of the army and protect it from assault as the main body passed through Cumberland Gap. I was further ordered to take command of all stragglers whom I found on the road. After proceeding some distance, I was informed by scouts that had been thrown forward that a company of from one hundred to one hundred and fifty bushwhackers had assembled in Williamsburg, a village of a few hundred inhabitants situated on the Cumberland River near its source, to resist our passing and to pick up stragglers. The column was immediately put in motion, and we went at a trot until we came to the opposite side of the river. Firing was commenced both on our front and flank; but it was soon over, for we charged them, and they broke and ran. About five of the bushwhackers (or home guards, as they styled themselves) were killed and many wounded.

I shall never forget an incident that occurred there. As we charged into the town the bushwhackers ran in every direction. Tom Gann, of Company C of my Regiment (which was formed afterwards), had pursued one of them beyond the town, when the fellow turned and fired upon him, killing his horse. Gann fired at the same time, but missed his aim. Neither of them having another load in reserve, the alternative was presented of "fighting it out on some other line." Gann at once seized a round stone and hurled it against the head of his adversary with such force as to break his skull, and he was left for dead.

On this route we were attacked as often as four or five times by bushwhackers. One day we were marching along quietly in column, not expecting an attack. The advance guard had passed, when suddenly a volley poured forth from the summit of a hill or mountain into the head of the column, wounding the man on my right and the horse on my left. We soon dispersed them, but it was a very annoying sort of warfare — that of the assassin shooting you in the back and running off.

After passing through the Gap, I reported to Colonel Wheeler, and I received from him an order to proceed to Knoxville. Reaching Knoxville about the 27th of October, it was understood that the army was moving to Murfreesboro, Tenn., as fast as the transportation permitted, and that the cavalry would move on leisurely to that point. At Murfreesboro Colonels Wheeler and Wharton each received their commissions as brigadier generals. These promotions were very well deserved, for each had won his spurs in that campaign.

In the early days of November, 1862, after the army had returned to Middle Tennessee, General Wharton moved out to the front and established his headquarters at Nolensville, a village in Williamson County, situated about sixteen miles from Nashville on one of the main roads leading out of the city. The Federal army then occupied Nashville with a large force under the command of Major General Rosecrans, who had superseded General Buell in Kentucky after the latter had given up the pursuit of General Bragg toward Cumberland Gap. General Rosecrans had turned and pressed his forces forward as rapidly as possible to Nashville. He was already in strong force there when General Bragg reached Murfreesboro. Upon the arrival of General Bragg at Murfreesboro, he at once set about reorganizing and recruiting his army. In November, 1862, I was notified through General Wharton of the organization of my Regiment and that I had been commissioned colonel of it by the War Department at Richmond.

CHAPTER XVIII.

Members of the Regiment Now Living.

THE following is a list of members now living (from latest information) who either surrendered with the Regiment or were honorably discharged therefrom for disability incurred during the war:

Field and Staff.

Col. Baxter Smith, Chattanooga, Tenn.; Adjt. George B. Guild, Nashville, Tenn.; Sergt. Maj. W. A. Rushing, Lebanon, Tenn.; Surgeon W. T. Delaney, Bristol, Va.; Assistant Surgeon J. T. Allen, Caney Springs, Tenn.; Acting Quartermaster R. O. McLean, Nashville, Tenn.; Acting Assistant Quartermaster Bob Corder, Williamson County, Tenn.; Acting Commissary First Lieut. J. T. Barbee, Sardis, Ky.

Company A.

Dr. Tom Allen, Caney Springs, Tenn.; Joe Yarbrough, Lewisburg, Tenn.; James Tippett, Greenville, Tex.; Thomas Sherron, Chapel Hill, Tenn.; William Edwards, Chapel Hill, Tenn.; Scott Davis, Lewisburg, Tenn.; Joe Yarbrough (second), Lewisburg, Tenn.; W. R. Wynn, Lewisburg, Tenn.; Polk Warner, Lewisburg, Tenn.; Ben Jobe, Paris, Tenn.; Jim Wilbern, Oklahoma; Melville Porter, McKenzie, Tenn.; William ("Dutch") Alexander, Chattanooga, Tenn.; Gid Alexander, New Orleans, La.

Company B.

Lieut. G. W. Carmack, Jonesboro, Tenn.; Henry Delaney, Bristol, Va.; Abe McClelland, Bluff City, Tenn.; W. C. Ingles, Knoxville, Tenn.; Dr. W. T. Delaney, Bristol, Va.

Company C.

Lieut. R. L. Scruggs, Stonewall, Tenn.; Lieut. Samuel Scoggins, Nashville, Tenn.; Pat Moss, Smith County, Tenn.; Ike Evans, Smith County, Tenn.; Dave Shipp, Smith County, Tenn.; William Bell, Big Spring, Tenn.; Sam Flippin, Birmingham, Ala.; Don Flippin, Smith County, Tenn.; Thomas Sanders, Nashville, Tenn.; Bob Grissim, Smith County, Tenn.

Company D.

First Lieut. Robert Bone, Texas; Second Lieut. J. T. Barbee, Sardis, Ky.; Third Lieut. J. A. Arnold, Lebanon, Tenn.

I feel that I ought to add here that Lieutenant Bone was one of the best and most active officers we had. He was always to be found in the forefront of the battle, and was wounded several times. In one of the last battles we had he was captured by the enemy; and while he was being carried to Johnson's Island with other prisoners he leaped from the train, making his escape into Canada, and was fortunate enough to get transportation upon a blockade runner coming into Charleston, S. C., reporting back to his regiment in four weeks after being captured. I am not positive that he is living to-day, but he was living in Texas when last heard from, more than a year ago.

Company E.

First Lieut. H. L. Preston, Woodbury, Tenn.; Third Lieut. John Fathera, Woodbury, Tenn.; N. Bony Preston, Woodbury, Tenn.; Thomas Vinson, Henry Gillam, William Wood, Warren Cummings, Al Kennedy, William Davis, N. A. Mitchell, I. Y. Davis, Eph Neely, R. S. Spindle, W. D. Coleman, John

Fourth Tennessee Cavalry Regiment. 241

Knox, John H. Wharton, B. F. Pinkerton, I. W. Stewart, Reese Hammons, John Hayes.

COMPANY F.

Lieutenant Williamson, Kentucky; W. H. Davis, Dallas, Tex.; J. H. Davis, Martha, Tenn.; Zack Thompson, Shelbyville, Tenn.

COMPANY G.

Capt. J. W. Nichol, Murfreesboro, Tenn.; Lieut. F. A. McKnight, Sergt. W. R. Fowler, Corp. I. C. Carnahan, L. M. Roberts, D. D. Murray, S. M. McGill, W. P. Gaither, L. L. Gaither, T. A. Gaither, S. M. McKnight, Robert Patrick, A. C. Good, I. F. Good, I. E. Neely, N. I. Ivie, W. H. Taylor, John Nugent, Houston Miller, L. W. Jarnigan, A. H. Youree, I. C. Coleman, W. W. Gray, B. L. Sagely, E. Bynum, E. H. Murrey, H. N. Jones, C. W. Moore, Calvin Brewer, James Love, Bob Knox.

Capt. J. W. Nichol, of Company G, says that of those living at this time, sixteen of them were young men on their way to join his company when the surrender occurred. The following are the circumstances in the case: Some weeks before the surrender, in 1865, he had sent his first lieutenant, Dave Youree, a most excellent and reliable officer, to Cannon and Rutherford Counties, Tenn., to obtain recruits. Just before the surrender Youree was returning to the command with the sixteen young men who had enlisted in said counties and whom he had sworn into the company and Regiment. Upon reaching the State of Georgia on their way to join the Regiment, then in North Carolina, they met General Forrest and his command and were informed

16

of the condition of the Confederate army. At General Forrest's suggestion, they remained with him, participated in his engagements around Selma, Ala., and surrendered with General Forrest's command, receiving their paroles at Gainesville, Ala., in May, 1865, as members of Company G, Fourth Tennessee Regiment. The sixteen young men are certainly entitled to be named in the list of living in Company G at this time, for they gave the best evidence of their manhood and patriotism by leaving voluntarily their homes behind the lines under the forlorn and desperate circumstances surrounding them and the Confederate army.

COMPANY H.

J. C. Ivey, Clear Lake, Tex.; Sam H. Bennett, Jasper, Tenn.; John Davis, Jasper, Tenn.; William T. Warren, Dayton, Tenn.; Zebulon Ballew, Sequatchie Valley, Tenn.; Billy Phelps, Sequatchie Valley, Tenn.; Robert Phelps, Sequatchie Valley, Tenn.

I have just received a letter from J. C. Ivey, of Company H, giving me the foregoing list of his company. I want to thank him again for the interest and assistance he has given me in preparing the facts for this narrative of the Regiment, and I feel that I ought to make his letter a part of the narrative. The letter is as follows:

CLEAR LAKE, TEX., October 16, 1912.

Maj. George B. Guild, Nashville, Tenn.

My Dear Adjutant and Comrade: Your letter came in due time, and this is the first opportunity I have had to answer your question in regard to those still living of Company H. There were thirty-four who were surrendered at Charlotte, N. C. I shall never forget that sorrowful day when we gave up our guns. That morning our beloved General Wheeler came to our Regiment and announced that we were a subjugated people and, while the tears were flowing from his eyes, advised us to return home and make as good citizens as we had soldiers and all would come out right. So far as I know, not one of those that were with us in the closing of this sad drama ever went wrong in any way. As for those that absented themselves, I have had no communication with any of them.

I remain your old comrade, J. C. IVEY.

COMPANY I.

Lieut. John W. Storey, Forest City, Ark.; B. P. Harrison, Albany, Ky.; Joel Brown, Glasgow, Ky.; Z. T. Crouch, Bellbuckle, Tenn.; Dr. Henry Sienknecht, Oliver Springs, Tenn.; John Hall, Tennessee; Isaac Ford, Rome, Tenn.; Orville I. Moate, Washington, D. C.; Lieut. William H. Hildreth, Alvarado, Tex.; John N. Simpson, Dallas, Tex.; William Wallace, Texas; Jeff Boles, Phœnix, Ariz.; Henry Gatewood, Ennis, Tex.

COMPANY K.

Frank Anderson, Nashville, Tenn.; Joe Miller, Lebanon, Tenn.; Hal Shutt, Lebanon, Tenn.; Bryant Goodrich, Nashville, Tenn.; James Thomas, Los Angeles, Cal.

I cannot hear of a single one of Company L who is alive to-day.

Some of the foregoing were young men just arriving at maturity and came out to the Regiment from Tennessee (then occupied by Federal forces) at the peril of their lives and joined it when the cause was a forlorn hope indeed. Of this class

244 Fourth Tennessee Cavalry Regiment.

Capt. Frank A. Moses, the Special Examiner on the State Confederate Pension Board, had occasion to say in his annual report to the Confederate Association of Bivouacs and Camps at Shelbyville recently:

> Comrades, it was easy for you and me to go out in 1861 or 1862, when the bright flags rippled in the breezes, the bands played "Dixie," and the girls waved their handkerchiefs, bidding us Godspeed; but when the dark days came and the flags were tattered and blood-stained, when the bands were playing the "Dead March" and the noble women mourned the death of loved ones, it was not so easy. When the old men and the boys in 1864 picked up the guns that had been thrown down by the quitters and stepped into our depleted ranks, they showed their faith by their works, and they are entitled to all honor.

I take occasion to add that I have been intimately associated with Captain Moses on the Pension Board for twenty years. He is most efficient in the position he occupies. He joined the Confederate army when but a boy. After engaging in the battle of Chickamauga, his regiment (the Sixty-Second Tennessee Infantry) was sent with Gen. Bushrod Johnson's brigade to the Army of Northern Virginia. He was severely wounded at the battle of Drewry's Bluff, on the James River, below Richmond; and after convalescing from his wound he reported to his command at Petersburg, and surrendered with General Lee at Appomattox on the 9th of April, 1865.

First Lieut. Rice McLean, of Company A, an

elegant gentleman and brave officer, was in command of his company most of the time, especially during the latter part of the war. His captain, Dave Alexander, was the oldest man in the Regiment and was much disabled by wounds. Lieutenant McLean was frequently called upon to perform the most hazardous and important duties, which he did with dispatch and to the highest satisfaction of the commanding officer. None stood higher in the Regiment or was more respected for his fidelity as a soldier. He was most amiable in character and in kindly comrádeship toward his fellow soldiers. He was wounded several times in battle. He died a few years ago in Kentucky, where he had lived since the close of the war. I could not resist the opportunity of saying a word regarding my warm personal friend, Rice McLean. He was a brother of the wife of Capt. Tom Hardison, one of Nashville's most worthy and honorable citizens.

Lieut. J. W. Storey, who was in command of Company I at the surrender, writes me that I should speak of the killing of Eb Crozier, of his company, who was a most intelligent, lovable man, and a brave soldier during the entire war. He received his parole of honor with the rest of the Regiment at Charlotte, N. C., May 3, 1865, and started home with us; but before reaching Sweetwater, Tenn., he took the road to the right to go to his home in Upper East Tennessee, which he had not visited for years. Upon reaching home, he was brutally murdered by a band of Union bushwhackers, with his parole of honor in his pocket, the ink with which it was written being hardly dry upon the paper. A more dastardly act was never perpetrated. His name has been placed among the killed in battle of his company, and I am sure that the reader will say that it rightfully belongs there, together with any other honor that could be attached to his memory.

Capt. James H. Britton, of Company K, was a native of Lebanon, Tenn., and was educated at Cumberland University, where he graduated with highest honors as a civil engineer. He was first lieutenant of the "Cedar Snags," of which Paul F. Anderson was captain. When the Fourth Tennessee Cavalry Regiment was organized, the company became a part of it. Captain Anderson became lieutenant colonel and Lieutenant Britton was made captain of Company K, both continuing as such until the surrender of the army, in 1865, at Greensboro, N. C. During the greater part of the war Company K was the escort of the commanding general. Captain Britton was a faithful, brave, and intelligent officer. He and his company were well known to the Army of Tennessee by the important duties that they were called upon to do in carrying orders to different parts of the field, frequently where the battle raged fiercest and hottest. The company's killed and wounded was heavy, as will

Fourth Tennessee Cavalry Regiment. 247

be seen on pages 165 and 166. Soon after the war Captain Britton moved to Texas, where he was successful as a business man and accumulated quite a fortune. He died there many years ago, a public-spirited, most worthy citizen. Dr. R. L. C. White and Wat Weakley, who were well-known citizens of Nashville, Tenn., were soldiers in this company, having joined it when it was first organized, and served throughout the war.

I have received from a friend the following record of Capt. J. W. Nichol prior to his company's being attached to the Fourth Tennessee Cavalry Regiment, which I take pleasure in making a part of this narrative:

Capt. J. W. Nichol was born and reared near Readyville, Rutherford County, Tenn., February 26, 1839. He entered the Confederate service at Murfreesboro, Tenn., May 21, 1861, as a lieutenant in Captain Wood's Company H, Joe B. Palmer's Eighteenth Tennessee Regiment, serving in same until a few days before the first battle at Fort Donelson, February, 1862. On a march from Bowling Green, Ky., we left him, sick of measles, at Russellville, Ky.; therefore he was not in the fight at Fort Donelson, where the Eighteenth Tennessee Regiment was captured and sent to prison. He was sent back with the sick to Bowling Green, thence to Nashville and Murfreesboro. At Murfreesboro he reported to Gen. A. S. Johnston, who directed him to get together all the members of the Eighteenth Tennessee Regiment who might be at home on sick furlough, also any who might have made their escape from prison, organizing them into a company or battalion, and connect the same with some other regiment. But before Captain Nichol could do this General Johnston, with his army, moved to Shelbyville, where Nichol reported to him again, informing him that he had met a number of the command who desired to join other regiments instead of forming a new command. General Johnston directed him to assign these men to any desired company until the Eighteenth should be exchanged. Nichol then, with nine others of the Eighteenth Tennessee, procured horses and fell back with General Johnston to Corinth, Miss., where they attached themselves to General Buckner's old escort, a Kentucky company commanded by Captain Kerr, who had made their escape from Fort Donelson and were serving as an escort for General Hardee. Nichol served as a private soldier with this company until after the battle of Corinth, April 6, 7, 1862. Some time after this battle he went to General Beauregard's headquarters (General Johnston having been killed in the engagement on April 6), and asked permission to go into Middle Tennessee and make up a cavalry company, which request was granted. With considerable difficulty he made his way to the neighborhood of his old home, there being Federal troops, stationed at Murfreesboro, who were scouting the surrounding country frequently. On one occasion Captain Unthanks, with a Yankee company of seventy-two men, came out from Murfreesboro to Readyville (Captain Nichol's old home), and went on to Woodbury and McMinnville on a scouting expedition. Colonel Starnes, commanding the Fourth Tennessee Cavalry, was near McMinnville and, upon learning of the scouting party headed by Captain Unthanks, moved into McMinnville in a few hours, and made inquiry for a man fully acquainted with the roads leading therefrom. Captain Nichol, who was just in from Corinth, Miss., reported to Colonel Starnes that he was conversant with all the roads leading to Murfreesboro. Leaving McMinnville late in the afternoon, Colonel Starnes and his men reached Woodbury about daylight of the next day, finding that Captain Unthanks had stopped there to feed his horses and had just left. Instantly pursuing, Starnes caught them at Readyville (Nichol's old home), eating breakfast, Captain Unthanks and most of his men being at Major Tallay's (the old Ready residence). Starnes was upon them be-

Fourth Tennessee Cavalry Regiment. 249

fore they were aware, killing three and capturing all except two others, who made their escape to Murfreesboro. Captain Nichol was then engaged in making up his company. Gen. Bedford Forrest passed through Readyville July 13, 1862; and Nichol, with a few unorganized men, fell in line and proceeded to Murfreesboro, where they participated in the first fight at Murfreesboro, in which they were victorious, taking all the prisoners to McMinnville to parole them. From there Nichol proceeded to Readyville, where he made up his company. About this time, learning of the approach of General Bragg toward Middle Tennessee, he, with about seventy unarmed young boys and men, riding all night, passing through Liberty, the home of Stokes and Blackburn (Yankee bushwhackers), got safely through to Sparta just in time to meet Bragg on his march into Kentucky. General Polk took Nichol's company for a time as couriers. Soon afterwards they were ordered to report to Maj. J. R. Davis, commanding a battalion of cavalry, and were in the fight at Perryville, Ky., fighting every day until they reached Cumberland Gap, losing several men. Thence they went to Murfreesboro, in which battle they were in Davis's Battalion. Shortly after this Smith's Fourth Tennessee Regiment was formed, composed of Smith's Battalion and Davis's Battalion. Immediately after this formation Wheeler and Forrest were ordered to Fort Donelson, where Nichol received his first serious wound. He was in all other engagements until the close of the war, being dangerously wounded at Bentonville, N. C., the last general engagement of the war. He surrendered at Greensboro, N. C., with Gen. Joseph E. Johnston's army, and was paroled at Charlotte, N. C., April 26, 1865.

When Colonel Smith returned, on exchange, from Johnson's Island Prison, just before the battle of Averyboro, N. C., he at once assumed command of the brigade as senior colonel. Adjt. George B. Guild became his adjutant general, and Capt. J. R.

Lester, of Company F, became his inspector general, all of them serving in this capacity till the surrender of the army at Greensboro, N. C., April 26, 1865. The coming of Colonel Smith created a scene of rejoicing with the Regiment, as it had created one of pronounced sorrow when he had been captured. The men pressed around him to show him the joy and pleasure it afforded. He was called upon to make a talk, when he expressed to them the pleasure it gave him to be with them again after his long, weary, and dark night as a prisoner in a Northern fortress. He said the saddest part of it was that he missed many familiar faces who were camping to-day on Fame's battle ground, and but a remnant remained of what they had been; that he had learned from time to time, as other prisoners came in, of the glorious record they were making and had made as soldiers. He expressed his pride in them, and said that their names would be remembered by grateful countrymen. Choking for utterance and in tears, he sat down. A few minutes after this the order was given to mount, and the brigade marched away to take part in the battle of Averyboro, N. C. A very interesting incident occurred before the foregoing took place. The Regiment had learned that his name had been registered for exchange and were expecting him. At the battle of Fayetteville, N. C., a few weeks before, Lieutenant Massengale had been killed, and his horse, which was a most excellent one, a rich bay, evidencing the qualities of a thoroughbred, was in the hands of a relative. It was proposed to purchase the horse for Colonel Smith when he reported, which was done. The men paid the relative $2,600 for the horse, which was christened "Lieut. Joe Massengale" in memory of his gallant rider who was killed upon his back while leading a charge in the fight with Kilpatrick's forces. Colonel Smith rode this horse in the battles that occurred afterwards and until the surrender. He brought "Joe Massengale" home with him. After this the horse was conspicuous as a part of all the reunions that took place, and was named the regimental mascot, by which name he was called until he died, in his twenty-sixth year.

. . . .

It has been assumed that the loss of life chargeable to the War between the States was over one million individuals. The number of great battles fought and the deadliness of the conflict are without a parallel in all modern history. In the Dark Ages of the world it frequently transpired that the victors assumed the divine right to massacre the defeated with fire and sword. We had a reminder of what that meant in the march to the sea and in the raids through the valleys of Virginia with a well-defined smell of fire and destruction about them. Truly it has been said that every messenger from the front told of the wreck of a living hope, and every home of both the North and South was made a house of mourning. But my object in giving the following incident is particularly to refute what has sometimes been unjustly said about the Confederate army as a band of slaveholders.

About the beginning of the war there lived in an adjoining county a young farmer who was a substantial, intelligent, and industrious citizen. By his energy he had accumulated means to buy a small hilly farm and erected upon it a plain but neat cottage, where he and his young wife lived. He had no farm help but a younger brother. In the fall of 1861 he and his brother enlisted in the Confederate army. His aged father and mother came to live with the wife, and in a short time the Tennessee regiment to which he and his brother were attached was ordered to the Army of Northern Virginia. The younger brother was killed the day Gen. Bob Hatton fell at Seven Pines, near Richmond, Va., in 1862. The old mother died in a short time after hearing of the death of her baby boy, as she affectionately called him. In 1863 the older brother was desperately wounded at Gettysburg in the charge of Archer's Tennessee Brigade on Cemetery Hill and taken a prisoner by the enemy. He was reported killed in action by his comrades, and was so reported on the rolls of his company during the remainder of the war. In fact, his

Fourth Tennessee Cavalry Regiment. 253

leg had been shattered by a cannon ball, and it was hastily amputated above the knee when he was sent to Rock Island Prison. The shock from the wound, exposure, and want of attention impaired his health, making him a patient of the prison hospital until the war ended. His wife, on learning of his death, sickened and died of a broken heart, it is said. The old father, having been left alone, went off to Kentucky to live with a married daughter. Marauding parties burned and destroyed the fences around the little farm, and the house was ruined and broken down. Nothing was left to remind one of the happy home it once had been.

Such was the health of the soldier that he was not discharged from the Rock Island hospital until some three months after the surrender of the Confederate armies, when he was paroled and permitted to return to his home. Upon reaching his home depot, in the first days of September, 1865, good-hearted Tom Day furnished him a horse to go out to his home. We will not attempt to depict his feelings on seeing the devastation that was spread before him upon reaching home. He sought the house of a neighbor, where he was told in sympathetic words the sad, sad story. He had not been able to write himself during his year or more as a prisoner; and confiding it to others, they had failed either willfully or negligently to do so. He listened in a dazed state of mind to the information imparted to him by his friend, but spoke not a word, remaining silent during the evening. As the lengthening shadows of the setting sun grew longer, he arose, saying that he would go down home again. He was asked to wait till morning and take a good night's rest, to which he gave no heed, hobbling off on his crutches in that direction. He did not return that night, and the next morning at the breakfast table the neighbor announced that he would go down and see if he could hear anything of his friend. On approaching the house, he found the door slightly ajar. Pushing it open, to his horror he beheld the soldier stretched upon the bare floor—dead. He, too, had died of a broken heart. The next day he was buried by a few sorrowing friends by the side of his wife, at the Old Salem Camp Ground, where his rude forefathers sleep.

The wrecks created along its pathway by a state of war are indeterminable. The destruction of property, public and private, is its natural consequence. Nor does its blighting effect end upon the battle field, but drags into its maelstrom of death the innocent, the helpless, and the unprotected. Truly can it be said that war makes countless thousands mourn.

These two young men were a type of the soldiery of which the Confederate armies were composed. They had no particular property rights to fight for; they owned no slaves; they were not personally interested in the slavery question. The doctrine of State rights had been the policy of the government since its existence. The Constitution and the laws made thereunder recognized it, and the Supreme Court of the United States in numerous decisions had sustained them. These were to be set at naught by force of arms, their country invaded, and their people to be subjugated. To prevent this they risked their lives and their all. Rebels they were in the sense that their forefathers had been, but patriots in the cause of freedom and in their efforts to preserve the inalienable rights of the citizen.

APPENDIX.

APPENDIX.

A.

AN extract from a letter of Gen. Marcus J. Wright to Thomas Nelson Page, author of "Robert E. Lee the Southerner," dated September 26, 1907, says:

From all reliable data that could be secured, it has been estimated by the best authorities that the strength of the Confederate armies was about 600,000 men, and of this number not more than two-thirds were available for active duty in the field. The necessity of guarding a long line of exposed seacoast and of maintaining permanent garrisons at different posts on inland waters and at numerous other points deprived the Confederate army in the field of an accession of strength. The large preponderance of Federal forces was manifest in all the important battles and campaigns of the war. The largest force ever assembled by the Confederates was at the Seven Days' fight around Richmond.

General Lee's report showed 80,835 men present for duty when the movement against General McClellan commenced, and the Federal forces numbered 115,240.

At Antietam the Federals had 87,164, and the Confederates had 35,255.

At Fredericksburg the Federals had 110,000, and the Confederates had 78,110.

At Chancellorsville the Federals had 131,661, of which number only 90,000 were engaged, and the Confederates had 57,212.

At Gettysburg the Federals had 95,000, and the Confederates had 44,000.

Fourth Tennessee Cavalry Regiment. 259

At the Wilderness the Federals had 141,160, and the Confederates had 63,981.

In the six battles named the Confederates were victorious in four of them, while the Federals were victors in one, and one was a drawn battle.

From the latter part of 1862 until the close of the war in 1865 there was a constant decrease of the numerical strength of the Confederate army. On the other hand, the records show that during that time the Federal army was strengthened to the extent of 363,390 men.

In April, 1865, the aggregate of present and absent showed the strength of the Confederate army to be about 275,000. Of this number, 65,387 were in Federal military prisons and 52,000 were absent by reason of disability and other causes. Deducting the total of these two numbers (117,387) from 275,000, we have 157,613 as showing the full effective strength of the Confederate army at the close of the war.

Gen. Marcus J. Wright has been for many years in charge of the Confederate Archives Department at Washington, D. C., including the muster rolls of the Confederate army, and is the best authority upon the subject he writes about.

The able editor of the New Orleans *Picayune*, in a recent editorial upon the strength of the Confederate army, says:

In the War between the States the official rolls of the Northern army show a total enlistment of 2,850,000 men. Allowing 700,000 men for the South—which would be the extreme limit for a white population of 6,000,000, of which 3,000,000 were women and more than 2,000,000 males under age, not to mention the 200,000 Southern men who went into the Union army and the men past military age and disabled—it would have been impossible for the South to have had more than 700,000 on its rolls, and these fought four to one. That these smaller numbers could inflict such heavy loss upon the superior numbers of their antagonists made it necessary, not only that they should have been ably led, but that they should have fought desperately and exhibited extraordinary powers of endurance, all of which they did up to the highest mark. By the records of modern warfare their performances have never been equaled, much less surpassed.

B.

"No step could have given more aid and comfort to the North or have been more disastrous to the South than the removal of General Johnston. Abroad it satisfied the anxious nations of Europe that the South was at her last gasp and established their hitherto vacillating policy in favor of the Union cause, and the Southern cause thereafter steadily declined to its end. The destruction of Hood's army at Nashville removed the only force capable of blocking the way of Sherman across the South and left him free to march to the sea and, having got in touch with the fleet there, continue through the Carolinas, marking his way with a track of devastation which has been likened to that made when Saxe carried fire and sword through the Palatinate." (See pages 63, 64 of "Robert E. Lee the Southerner," by Thomas Nelson Page.)

The North was enabled to recruit her armies by drafting all the men she needed, and her command of the sea gave her Europe as a recruiting ground. On October 17, 1863, the President of the United

Fourth Tennessee Cavalry Regiment. 261

States ordered a draft for 300,000 men. On February 1, 1864, he called for 500,000; and on March 14, 1864, he issued an additional call for 200,000 more "to provide an additional reserve for all contingencies." The South was almost spent. Her spirit was unquenched and was, indeed, unquenchable; but her resources, both of treasury and of men, were exhausted. Her levies for reserves of all men between fifteen and sixty drew from President Davis the lament that she was grinding the seed corn of the Confederacy.

C.

Gen. W. T. Sherman, in his report of May 4, 1864, says:

The Confederate army at my front at Dalton, Ga., comprised, according to the best authority, about 45,000 men, commanded by Joseph E. Johnston, who was equal in all the elements of generalship to Lee and who was under instruction from the war power at Richmond to assume the offensive northward as far as Nashville. But he soon discovered that he would have to conduct a defensive campaign. Coincident with the movement of the Army of the Potomac, as announced by telegraph, I advanced from our base at Chattanooga with the Army of the Ohio, 13,550 men; the Army of the Cumberland, 60,773 men; the Army of the Tennessee, 24,405 men (grand total, 98,707 men); and 254 guns.

INDEX.

Adams, 117.
Aiken, J. A., 164.
Alexander, D. W., 9, 156.
Alexander, Gid, 239.
Alexander, William, 239.
Allen, Dr. Tom, 9, 239.
Allen, T., 159.
Allen, T. J., 165.
Allen, W., 159.
Allison, Henry, 156.
Anderson, A. A., 157.
Anderson, DeWitt, 10, 166.
Anderson, Frank, 166, 243.
Anderson, Lieut. Col. P. F., 9, 54, 182.
Arnold, J. A., 10, 159, 240.
Arnold, James, 156.
Armstrong, J., 160.
Atkins, Fentress, 165.
Austin, Levi, 164.
Avants, H., 157.
Avants, N., 157.

Baily, Jonathan, 164.
Baker, J. N., 158.
Ballew, Zeb, 242.
Barbee, Lieutenant, 10, 159, 239, 240.
Barnes, Joe, 165.
Barton, Jack, 166.
Beard, Lieut. Charles, 9.
Beauregard, General, 172.
Bell, J. C., 156.
Bell, John, 158.

Bell, P., 164.
Bell, W., 166, 240.
Bennett, James, 163.
Bennett, Moses, 163.
Bennett, S. H., 242.
Blackburn, Captain, 46.
Bledsoe, A., 164.
Bledsoe, Capt. Robert, 10, 164.
Bledsoe, Maj. Scott, 9, 125, 184.
Bone, Capt. William, 9.
Bone, Lieut. Bob, 10, 159, 240.
Bowles, Jeff, 243.
Bowman, John, 165.
Bowman, Lieut. Foster, 10, 165.
Bragg, General, 9, 14, 57.
Brandon, J. A., 162.
Breckenridge, General, 23, 140.
Brewer, C., 241.
Britton, Capt. James, 10, 246.
Brown, Joel, 243.
Brown, R., 165.
Burford, Ben, 158.
Burgess, Lieutenant, 10, 161.
Burke, James, 161.
Bushong, D., 157.
Bynum, E., 241.
Bynum, W. M., 162.

Caline, William, 157.
Carder, Jack, 161.
Carmack, D. C., 157.

Carmack, Lieutenant, 10.
Carmack, Lieut. Gid, 157, 239.
Carter, General, 117.
Cato, Joe, 158.
Chapman, Bennett, 9.
Cheatham, General, 23.
Chenyworth, Colonel, 44.
Christian, Major, 46.
Claiborne, General, 23, 116.
Coleman, J. C., 162.
Cook, Colonel, 46.
Cook, Col. Ed, 65.
Cooper, I., 162.
Corbett, W., 10.
Corder, Bob, 9, 239.
Cox, James, 157.
Crockett, Frank, 156.
Crouch, Zack T., 243.
Crozier, Lieut. E., 125, 245.
Cunningham, Frank, 10.
Curren, George, 158.
Curren, W. J., 156.

Dark, James, 156.
Davis, James, 156.
Davis, J. H., 241.
Davis, John, 242.
Davis, President, 66, 138.
Davis, Robert, 131.
Davis, Robert A., 165.
Davis, Scott, 239.
Davis, W. H., 241.
Deadman, 158.
Deason, William, 165.
Delaney, Dr. W. T., 9, 157, 239.
Delaney, Henry, 157, 239.
Dibrell, General, 39, 71, 108.

Dillard, J., 161.
Dillard, John, 158.
Dillon, S., 159.
Doak, Tom, 160.
Donnell, R. O., 158.
Doughtry, James, 162.
Douglass, C. M., 164.
Douglass, John, 65.
Dunn, J. F., 162.
Durham, A. D., 164.

Edwards, Joe, 158.
Edwards, William, 239.
Elliott, Lieutenant, 10.
Evans, Capt. Mark, 234.
Evans, Ike, 240.
Ewing, Col. Andrew, 59.

Fagan, Lon, 156.
Fagan, Tom, 156.
Farnsworth, George, 166.
Fathera, Lieutenant, 10, 160, 240.
Fields, W., 10.
Finney, Sergeant, 9.
Flippin, Don, 240.
Flippin, H. L., 158.
Flippin, S., 240.
Floridy, T., 159.
Ford, Isaac, 243.
Forrest, General, 11, 16.
Fowler, Sergt. W. R., 162, 241.

Gaither, L. L., 241.
Gaither, T. A., 241.
Gaither, W. P., 162, 241.
Gann, Bob, 9.
Gann, H., 158.

Gann, John, 159.
Gant, William, 163.
Gatewood, Henry, 243.
Gentry, James, 156.
Gillihan, E., 158.
Glover, H. C.
Glover, S., 10, 163.
Goad, William, 164.
Godges, Rufus, 164.
Godsey, T., 163.
Godsey, W. J., 157.
Goodrich, Bryant, 243.
Gordon, John, 162.
Grady, Henry, 110.
Granbery, General, 117.
Gray, W. W., 162.
Green, Allen, 163.
Green, James, 158.
Green, Lieutenant, 10.
Grissim, Bob, 240.
Grissim, M. (Q. M.), 9, 155, 158.
Guild, G. B., 54, 76, 125, 239.

Hall, John, 243.
Hampton, General, 112.
Hancock, Ed, 165.
Hardee, General, 65, 127, 133.
Hare, Joe, 160.
Hare, Tim, 156.
Hargrove, N., 156.
Harris, John, 162.
Harrison, Colonel, 125.
Harrison, Porter B., 165, 243.
Harron, H. H., 163.
Hawkins, E. J., 160.
Hayes, J., 241.
Hearn, James, 165.

Hearn, R., 165.
Hendrix, W. W., 9.
Henlen, J. A., 157.
Henry, Lieutenant, 10.
Herndon, Liter, 127.
Hicks, E. and W.
Hildreth, Lieutenant, 10, 243.
Hill, L., 165.
Hill, Mike, 165.
Hilton, J. B., 164.
Hogan, Lieutenant, 10, 158.
Hood, General, 62, 68, 116, 119, 177.
Hopkins, John, 156.
Horton, Jesse, 165.
Hughes, James, 162.
Hull, 157.
Hume, General, 124.
Hutton, Polk, 156.

Ingles, Capt. C. H., 9.
Ingles, W. C., 239.
Ivey, J. C., 164, 242.
Ivie, H. J., 162.
Ivie, N. I., 241.

Jackson, Dan, 163.
James, J. E., 162.
Jarman, H., 159.
Jarmin, Captain, 46.
Jarnigan, L. W., 241.
Jobe, Ben, 239.
Johnson, Ab.
Johnson, T., 159.
Johnston, Gen. A. S., 172.
Johnston, Gen. Joseph E., 59, 65, 126, 148, 172, 173.
Jones, D. C., 162.

Fourth Tennessee Cavalry Regiment. 265

Jones, H. N., 241.
Jones, J. E., 162.
Jowett, Cullom, 164.
Joyner, Major, 135.

Kennedy, Al, 240.
Kennedy, A. W., 160.
King, M. T., 157.
Kirk, B., 161.
Kirkpatrick, Captain, 47.
Knox, Bob, 241.
Knox, William, 159.

Lee, General, 172.
Lester, Capt. J. R., 10, 13, 161.
Lester, T., 157.
Lester, William, 161.
Light, Lieut. William, 10, 164.
Lindamond, James, 157.
Longstreet, General, 33.
Love, James, 241.
Lunn, W. F., 156.
Luttrell, J., 157.
Lyons, P. A., 156.

Magill, Walter, 163.
Mallard, J. R., 156.
Marlin, Jesse, 156.
Martin, Gid, 162.
Martin, R., 163.
Massengale, John.
Massengale, Lieut. Joe, 9, 143, 157.
Massengale, William, 163.
Mattern, H., 157.
McCall, John, 163.
McClelland, Abe, 157, 239.
McClelland, Edward, 240.
McDonough, James, 163.

McDowell, Jack, 165.
McGee, G. M., 158.
McGill, S. M., 241.
McKnight, Lieut. F. A., 162, 241.
McKnight, S. M., 241.
McLean, Lieut. Rice, 9, 156, 244.
McLean, R. O., 9, 156, 239.
McMillin, Capt., 24.
McNairy, Col. Frank, 16.
McNeilly, Rev. J. H., 191.
Miller, H., 162, 241.
Miller, Joe, 243.
Milton, C., 160.
Minnis, Adjt. J. A., 9, 18.
Minton, J., 158.
Mitchell, J., 160.
Mitchell, N., 160.
Mitchell, N. A., 240.
Mitchell, O. K., 163.
Moate, O. I., 243.
Modly, A., 158.
Mont, T., 159.
Moore, C. W., 241.
Moore, G. C., 10, 158.
Morrell, William, 157.
Morris, J. M., 164.
Moses, Capt. Frank, 244.
Moss, Pat, 240.
Mullinax, F., 159.
Murrey, E. H., 241.
Murrell, J. T., 157.
Murry, D. D., 241.

Nance, J. B., 9, 129.
Neal, William, 166.
Nealy, J., 160.

Neely, E., 240.
Neely, I. E., 241.
Neely, T., 160.
Neil, W. J., 156.
Nelson, Henry, 166.
Nevels, Ben, 156.
Newlan, Anderson.
Newsom, Joe, 165.
Nichols, Capt. J. W., 10, 132, 162, 241, 248.
Nugent, John, 241.

O'Dell, P., 157.
Odum, D., 159.
Oglesby, Nick, 156.
Orr, Lieut. J. N., 9.
Owens, Elias, 164.

Padgett, James, 164.
Pain, G. V. and William.
Parton, Capt. J. J., 10.
Patrick, A. R., 162.
Patrick, Robert, 241.
Paty, M., 158.
Pemberton, M., 159.
Phelps, Billy, 242.
Phelps, R., 242.
Phillips, J. M., 10, 159.
Phillips, W. H., 73, 161.
Pickett, J. M., 163.
Pickett, John, 163.
Polk, Lieutenant General, 64.
Poor, Pleasant, 165.
Porterfield, D., 160.
Powell, N., 159.

Preston, B. P., 160.
Preston, Lieut. H. L., 10, 143, 160, 240.
Price, John T., 9.

Raine, John, 166.
Rains, Gen. Jim, 13.
Ransom, C., 156.
Reed, James, 156.
Reid, B., 160.
Richerson, O., 159.
Ridley, Granville.*
Roberts, C. M., 162.
Roberts, L. M., 162, 241.
Robinson, Arch, 162.
Robinson, A. W., 162.
Robinson, Jesse, 162.
Robinson, M., 159.
Roder, A. L., 157.
Roland, A., 158.
Rushing, Joe A., 162.
Rushing, J. R., 160.
Rushing, Sergt. Maj. W. A., 9, 113, 239.
Russell, Lieut. H., 10.
Ryburn, J. S., 157.

Sagely, Lieut. J. A., 10, 162.
Sams, William, 157.
Sandifer, William, 156.
Scoggins, Lieut. Sam, 10, 134, 240.
Scruggs, Lieut. R. L., 10, 158, 240.
Shell, William, 163.

---

*Granville Ridley enlisted in the Regiment when sixteen years of age, while Wheeler was on his last raid into Tennessee in 1864, and served faithfully till the surrender.

Fourth Tennessee Cavalry Regiment. 267

Shumate, R., 163.
Shutt, Hal, 243.
Sienknecht, Dr. Henry, 243.
Simpson, J. N., 243.
Singleton, James, 165.
Slaughter, George, 156.
Smith, Col. Baxter, 9, 17, 18, 125, 130, 143, 186, 239, 273.
Smith, Jack, 163.
Smith, John, 165.
Smith, William, 164.
Snodgrass, J. Y., 157.
Spain, W. M., 162.
Spencer, Z., 156.
Stanton, Col. S. S., 61.
Starnes, Gen. James, 20.
Stearns, Colonel, 11.
Stewart, Gen. A. P., 62.
Stewart, J. A., 9, 17, 158.
Stone, William, 163.
Storey, Lieut. J. W., 10, 165, 243.
Strahl, General, 117.
Sullivan, T., 158.
Sullivan, W. S., 10.
Sutton, H., 164.

Tacket, Alex, 164.
Taylor, W. H., 241.
Thomas, James, 243.
Thompson, D., 164.
Thompson, James, 156.
Thompson, Z., 161, 241.
Tippett, Jim, 239.
Tittle, T. J., 160.
Todd, Alfred, 162.
Todd, Calep, 162.
Todd, Walker, 162.

Tolbert, D. W., 162.
Tomlinson, E., 158.
Trousdale, W., 158.
Turner, J. M., 156.

Vance, T., 160.
Van Trease, A., 165.
Vinson, T., 240.

Walker, Colonel, 65.
Walkup, L., 160.
Wallace, W., 243.
Waller, Sam, 156.
Warner, Polk, 239.
Warren, W. T., 242.
Warren, W. W., 163.
Watkins, Thomas, 164.
Watts, David, 156.
Weakley, Wat, 247.
Weaver, C., 159.
Webber, C. M., 162.
Wharton, General, 11, 27, 46.
Wharton, J. H., 241.
Wharton, Tobe, 166.
Wheeler, General, 11, 16, 69, 108, 150, 179.
White, Captain, 17.
White, Dr. R. L. C., 247.
White, M. M., 163.
Whitecotten, I., 163.
Wilbern, J., 239.
Williams, A., 164.
Williams, General, 97, 102.
Williams, James, 163.
Williamson, Lieutenant, 241.
Williamson, Lieut. James, 10.
Wilson, Billy, 156.

Winder, J. B., 164.
Witherspoon, D. C., 162.
Witherspoon, Sam, 162.
Wood, William, 157, 240.
Woods, C. C., 157.
Wyly, Capt. H. A., 10, 44, 161.
Wynn, W. R., 156, 239.

Yarbrough, Joe, 156, 239.
Young, Dock, 158.
Young, Gen. Bennett H., 204.
Youree, A. H., 241.
Youree, Frank, 162.
Youree, Lieut. Dave, 10, 162.
Youree, W. H., 162.

www.ingramcontent.com/pod-product-compliance
Lightning Source LLC
Chambersburg PA
CBHW050555170426
43201CB00011B/1698